Why Asking Donors For Money Causes Donors To Give Less

A team builder's guide to increasing what people give by 83% for nonprofits and those just willing to ask

Lindsay Walton

Dedicated to

All those who have done something that seemed more than a little crazy to other people in order to make the world a better place.

My husband, Nathan. Thank you for helping to make completing this project possible. 🖤

My son, Gabriel. You are more than enough motivation to try and help the world be the best it can be. The day you showed up my heart started wandering around outside my body. 🖤

ISBN: 978-1-7753276-2-2

TABLE OF CONTENTS

A NOTE ON WISDOM

I am responsible for choosing to write this book. You are responsible for choosing what you do with it. Make good choices.

WHO IS THIS BOOK FOR?

I encourage you to treat your journey through this book like a trip to the grocery store...

WHO IS THIS BOOK FOR?

This book is primarily about how to successfully gather the necessary resources to survive and how to gather additional resources in order to reach further than you ever thought possible. As a result, I think the majority of people and organizations in this world could find something of benefit within its pages.

The material was developed with the following in mind:

- Anyone relying on external support for their continued existence and ability to achieve their mission, whether through fundraising, grants, or other forms of asking.

- Non-profit organizations who are groups of people teamed up together, passionate about taking on a particular challenge, and who are working together to make the world a better place.

- Individuals who raise their own support in order to dedicate their time to making the world a better place either through working with an agency or working as an independent unit.

- Individuals who are passionate about seeing positive change happen around them and invest their efforts into supporting other people and organizations.

- Communities who are interested in seeing the needs of everyone within the community met through the sharing of resources.

- Individuals who are feeling the crunch of having too little resources, or have resources available to them that aren't the right kind needed right now (ex. students, families burdened with debt, seniors with limited resources for retirement, etc).

For simplicity of language the wording of the book is directed to non-profit organizations, however, it is equally beneficial to individuals and communities. Tools have been provided later in the book to help you apply the principles if you belong to any of the categories above.

Because non-profit organizations and communities come in so many shapes and sizes, and because all human beings and their circumstances are unique, it would be impossible to write the entire book in such a way that everything is applicable to everyone. So instead I encourage you to treat your journey through this book like a trip to the grocery store.

There will be some things that you've tried before but that can be tried in a new recipe. There will be new things that will be exciting to try for the first time. There will be things that could be really good if you add your own personal flavour, some things that look a little weird and fruity but are worth trying, and some things that you're wondering how they got on the shelf for consideration in the first place. It's all good. Wander the aisles. See what there is to see. Put in your cart the things that are going to make a positive difference for you or your organization now, tweaking them as you see fit. And leave the rest on the shelves to come back to another time if you wish.

The materials in this book are not a carved-in-stone, this-is-the-only-way-to-do-it template. Instead, everything here is a jumping off point, food for thought, and adaptable. If you'd like to connect with other people chewing over the material and figuring out how to best apply it to their circumstances you can hop on Facebook and join the Resource Campaign Community group.

If you're ready to see what's available to you then grab a cart!

THE HISTORY BEHIND THIS BOOK

All I could think was, "Do you have any idea what this rubber chicken can do? Do you have any idea what this chicken is capable of?"

THE HISTORY BEHIND THIS BOOK

"Nice to meet you, Lindsay! So, what do you do for a living?"

"I'm a team builder."

"…?"

I'm not going to lie. Sometimes I wish I were a flight attendant or a real estate agent because then when people ask what I do for a living I would stop getting blank stares. I usually intrigue people when I go on to explain that I provide programs and training that build people's core team skills, such as communication and problem-solving, so the teams they belong to can thrive. And I can usually get a smile when I share that also means I show up at people's workplaces, schools, camps or other organizations with a laptop and projector or a suitcase full of rubber chickens, whichever is needed at the time.

As a professional team builder, I am a *facilitator*. That means I take very seriously that I can create environments and experiences which enable participants to take away more from their time with me than I ever thought possible. In the end, what they *experienced* is going to speak so much louder than anything I said or any individual thing that I did, so it is very much worth my effort to be intentional about the kind of environment and experience I create.

One of my favourite examples is teaching first aid classes. First Aid Instructor is just one of many hats I wear and I teach the courses, not because I'm a medical professional or have interest in the medical field, but because it's such a powerful facilitation tool. Sure, I teach my participants about preventing cardiovascular disease and how to recognize the signs and symptoms of a heart attack. Sure, I instruct them on how to perform CPR and use an Automated External Defibrillator (AED). But when I create a physically and emotionally safe learning environment for a group of youth who have a history of violence so that they can complete a certification that will help them find stable employment after being released from jail… a world of magic starts to unfold.

These individuals, who have been told over and over that they are screw-ups and garbage, leave at the end of the course knowing they can save a life and that they have something valuable to offer the world. Those in the group who struggle with depression, anger, and fear related to past traumas gain more peace of mind because they have opportunity to replace old messages of "it's my fault" with "I did everything I could", and "what if it happens again" with "I know what to do, I can improve the situation". The change in self-esteem, self-worth, and confidence by the end of a two-day Standard First Aid course is dramatic. Participants are walking differently, holding themselves taller, prouder, and more calmly by the end of class. And they walk out of there with a certificate that is proof of the journey they went on and what they have to offer the world. That's what I love about teaching first aid. But to anyone who is not a facilitator, one of these classes may just look like a first aid course that was reasonably interesting and fun. Nothing more.

Facilitators around the globe use their super powers of creating multi-layered environments and experiences for many different purposes. Some are school teachers, team builders, high ropes course professionals, or dog-sledders. Some are corporate trainers, counsellors or psychiatrists. Some are sales professionals, greeters, or artists. Wherever they are applying their skill set they simply know that environment and experience *matter* and that once you set the ball in motion it's the participant who will take the experience where it needs to go and that will result in the greatest life-changing impact.

My formal training is spread across a number of fields. I originally entered university studying Theatre and English because my dream was to become a high school teacher of those subjects. However, I identified quickly that I loved to do those things for fun and that doing them for a living was sucking the life right out of them. I needed to figure out my future fast as several thousand dollars in tuition money was now on the line and I ended up finding myself heading in an unexpected direction. I started studying Recreation, Sociology, and Social Work because something about the courses offered in those departments spoke to me. After leaving the registrar's office, having changed my major and minors and leaving him with a puzzled look because of the strange soup mix of studies he thought I'd created, I was soon hit with a blinding revelation.

One of my elective recreation courses was on team building and the professor had us in the gym playing a combination of games that all used rubber chickens. He dropped an off-hand comment about one particular game being an icebreaker to help people get to know each other and it was like a pile of heavy golden puzzle pieces dropped from the sky and locked into place creating this amazing picture of what my future could look like. Social work is all about walking beside people who hurt and supporting them through their challenges while they heal and move forward. Sociology is all about studying human dynamics and why people do the weird things we do when we're together. Recreation is about creating opportunities for people to be together.

11

[Insert bright lights shining and angels singing]

I looked at the rubber chicken in my hand and was blown away. This tool could be used to play a game that would help people to get to know each other, bringing them closer together and beginning the process of building long-term relationships that could then sustain those people through dark times. For someone who is suicidal, having a single person willing to keep them company while they hurt can make the difference between life and death. In the big picture, icebreakers help to save lives. This chicken could save lives! All I could think was, "Do you have any idea what this rubber chicken can do? Do you have any idea what this chicken is capable of?"

I didn't know all the ins and outs yet of how it was going to happen, but I knew right then and there that I wanted to be a team builder. I wanted to use play and adventure-based activities to help bring people who were alone and isolated into strong teams and healthy communities that would act as vital support networks as we navigate life's challenges *together*.

My career has taken me in several interesting directions. I've been a high ropes professional, climbing trees for a living and using aerial elements as a tool for helping people learn how to work together, trust each other, and overcome their personal fears. I've been an outdoor educator using canoeing and archery to teach students that they are capable problem-solvers and able to achieve so much more if they ask questions and are willing to explore their world. And, after starting my own company, Open Door Development, in 2008 I am now primarily a team builder, trainer, and speaker. This means I travel to clients' sites to provide play-based team building programs, tailored presentations, and interactive classroom training in specific team skills such as conflict resolution, first aid, stress reduction, leadership, facilitation, and more.

I attribute a large portion of the success I've achieved in my field to a quirk I've had since I was a child and that helps to explain some of my earlier interest in teaching theatre. I am a people watcher. I remember sharing this with a class I was teaching and a woman audibly gasped and couldn't help asking, "you mean you *stalk* people?" I couldn't help but laugh out loud. No, I don't stalk people. But I do watch them. I can think of few greater things in life than to sit on a park bench with a cup of tea and good company and to watch the world go by.

Human beings are such beautifully diverse creatures in so many ways. I'm not just talking about skin colour, hair, eyes, clothing choices, etc. I'm talking about habits, quirks, mannerisms, and ways of moving. For example, have you ever noticed that every jogger holds their arms slightly differently? Jogging is jogging, right? Wrong! Look closely and you'll see open hands and clenched fists, arms kept bent at a perfect ninety degrees and arms that are flying about all over the place, arms pumping high and arms locked in at the side. My favourite was a gentleman whose combination of limp hands and tight elbows made it look like he was running like a velociraptor.

Even more complex to watch are humans interacting with other humans. We are crazy, amazing, complex communicators. We use our choice of words, tone of voice, facial expressions, and body language to send messages to each other and do it both consciously and subconsciously, intentionally and unintentionally.

People lean in towards what they are interested in, look upwards and involuntarily smile while accessing happy memories, and drop their chins when they are feeling shame. They bend subtly to avoid touching those they are uncomfortable with, avoid eye contact when they don't want to engage, and lift one side of their nose when they are disgusted by someone or something. They exhale more heavily if something you said resonated with them deeply, adjust their wedding ring while discussing their spouse when the relationship is strained, and so much more.

The patterns I saw emerging over the years as I continued to watch people have served me incredibly well as a facilitator because my observations of a group have helped me to shape their experience and to shape the questions I ask them. Good questions are critical because I am not a mind reader! One can *never* diagnose what someone else is thinking. But one can make an educated guess based on the human patterns being displayed and ask questions that help to determine if you're on the right track.

That participant just looked up and involuntarily smiled while talking about their grandmother. That's a perfect opportunity to say, "It seems like she has played an important part in your life. Do you have good memories of her?" This group of participants just had two people close the gap between their eyebrows and tilt their heads slightly to the side when I used the term 'peer orientation'. That's a perfect opportunity to stop and ask the group, "Are you familiar with the concept of peer orientation?" and expand with further detail before moving on.

Speaking and presenting are very much a conversation with the audience. I may be doing most of the talking, but there is an incredible amount of two-way communication as the audience provides visual and auditory cues. Individuals lean forward and lean backward, rest their chins in their hands, cross their arms, sit up straighter, sink in their seats, let out sighs, tilt their heads to the side, roll their eyes, nod, narrow their eyes, purse their lips, and smile. It helps me know who needs to be reengaged, what words or concepts to explain more in-depth, who has heard this a thousand times and needs some interesting new insight to spice this experience up for them, and who is chomping at the bit to know more. Motion within the audience is a tip to look over, see what kind of motion it is, and react accordingly. Following the waves of motion around the room makes it possible for your eye contact to be personal, the information you deliver of immediate value, and the message to the audience clear that you are *listening* to them even if they aren't speaking. This consistently results in feedback that this was one of the best presentation experiences they've had.

When I'm facilitating a play-based team building program I am more off to the side as I set an activity in motion and then get out of the way as the team takes over. As a fly on the wall while team members problem-solve and debrief there is an incredible amount of visual and auditory input. I find that watching a group of people interacting with each other is very much like watching a fireworks display. There is so much going on and it's beautiful and complex and makes up this grand whole in front of you. And for someone who is watching and listening carefully so they can gather information to shape debriefing questions and choose the next activity wisely, a twenty-minute challenge can result in a textbook worth of information on the team and its internal dynamics.

So, what does any of that have to do with this book?

My years of watching people from park benches and cafe terraces along with my years of experience within all the realms in which I facilitate have provided me with front row seats for tens of thousands of requests for help and the reactions those requests received. I have to tell you, the patterns found within those requests and responses are so incredibly interesting. Humans require different forms of help or different resources in order to overcome the various challenges they encounter. I have seen people ask others for help in the form of physical assistance (can you pull me up?), provision of direction (where do I go next?), clarification (are we allowed to step on this square?), reassurance (did I do the right thing?), a listening ear (can I talk with you for a bit?) and more. I have seen requests for help fulfilled immediately by the person asked, answered with some hesitation, and ignored or outright denied. Two people could ask the same team member for the exact same help, and that person will respond with assistance for one and not the other, with zero malice intended, and go on to provide different help when a later opportunity presents itself. Someone could ask a team member for help and they happily step forward but become instantly uncomfortable once it is clarified what kind of help was being solicited. A team member can want to help, and the chances of helping increase with the quality of the relationship, but the chances of helping drop significantly if the relationship is damaged or if they are being asked for a form of help that they are not interested in giving. And the form of help they are interested in giving depends on who is asking!

Communities are simply large teams and the same dynamic exists whether you are looking at an apartment building, neighbourhood, small town, or megacity. For the organizations and individuals who reach out to their communities for support in order to achieve their mission, they are surrounded by people who want to help! But they won't get the help they need if they are asking in a way that damages relationships or are asking for a form of help the person they are speaking to does not want to give.

I've watched canvassers in grocery stores, on street corners, and going door to door. I've been with friends in their homes when they happened to be opening their mail, spoken with people discussing recent interactions with a nonprofit, and wondered at the complete lack of resources available to help organizations get on a better track for asking for help. What many organizations don't realize is that what they are currently doing *is not working,* even if they are meeting or exceeding their financial goals! I see the eye rolls, raised nostrils, firm taps of the delete button, emphatic ripping up and tossing out of mail-outs, and hear the vocalized sounds of disgust. I can see the damaged relationships when organizations keep asking for money. And I can see the brightened eyes, the straighter posture, the leaning in, the focused drop of the eyebrows, the sudden tuning in of attention, the rotating of the head in order to have a direct line of sight, and the energy in the fingers when a person hears an opportunity to help that resonates with them. But many organizations aren't asking for that form of help and so the opportunity to receive it passes them by.

So many organizations have no idea how much help their communities want to offer them, or how critical the environment and experience they are creating when asking is. Or they don't know what clues and human patterns to look for to shape the questions they ask a donor in order to help identify exactly *how* that person wants to give.

I hope as a result of bundling together my insights about communities, asking for help, and resource gathering practices for your consideration that breakthrough and great things are waiting for you.

Cheers.

MATH CAN BE SNEAKY

Math does not always provide us with intuitively clear answers regarding campaign success when it comes to the human side of things because it all depends on *what numbers you're working with* and *how you crunch them*.

A DAY IN THE LIFE OF A DONOR

Everywhere you go there's a fundraising campaign happening. You read the morning newspaper and see ads for charitable lotteries. You get to work and are asked by your employer to donate a toonie if you want to wear jeans on Friday to support a local non-profit initiative. At lunch, you're approached by a co-worker asking if you'll sponsor them for a 5km race they're running in memory of their Mother. On your way home the radio reminds you to buy your tickets for the upcoming community event supporting x charity. You get home to open your mail (two requests from organizations suggesting making monthly donations) and check your email (another e-newsletter from that charity you donated to once). You try to relax by surfing the internet only to have your desired content surrounded by ads asking you to click to donate to this worthy cause now! You tuck your kids into bed and agree to go with them on the weekend to knock on doors to sell the muffin mix your son is supposed to be selling for school and the chocolate bars your daughter is supposed to be selling for her sports team. You may as well ask those same neighbours if they'd like to give towards the humanitarian trip you're going on six months from now that you're supposed to be raising your own support for. Lying in bed, thinking about what your bank account and credit card bills look like right now, you're considering starting a fundraiser for you...

It seems like everyone needs money, and that everyone wants yours!

Anyone who is asking for money has had it hammered home that they have significant competition for a donor's time, attention, and resources. They know that the tools they use to obtain a slice of what is available will make the difference between whether their financial spreadsheet has a + or - sign at the bottom. The tools can make the difference between whether or not an organization is able to keep its doors open. They can determine if a person is able to dedicate their lives to a cause they are passionate about or if that person has to sideline their passion for a time in order to make sure their basic needs are taken care of.

In our North American society, we've developed a mentality that it's a real achievement to have gathered what you need amidst all the competition. Fundraisers that achieve their financial goals are celebrated and held up as examples for others. Other individuals and organizations analyze their success looking at every nuance including what kinds of tools they used, what wording they used, what donors they reached out to, what partners they worked with, how they advertised, etc, etc, etc, and they try to emulate that success.

They also try to avoid the mistakes made by others so they can avoid repeating their failure. In addition to the stress of not having enough resources to sustain an endeavour, many experience a deep sense of personal shame if they don't achieve their financial goal. Nobody likes to feel that way and so we analyze the scenarios where organizations and individuals missed their mark. What kinds of tools did they use, what wording did they use, what donors did they reach out to, what partners did they work with, how did they advertise, etc, etc, etc.

Based on what I've seen, the individuals and organizations analyzing this information most intently are not within the non-profit organizations themselves but are instead from the for-profit realm. Because if they can tease out the secrets to success and how to avoid failure then they have a great product to sell! Non-profit organizations are a *huge* source of revenue for the for-profit realm!!!

After all their analyses the main conclusion that seems to have been derived is that when you approach people to ask them for support there are only two options for how they will respond. A person will either say 'yes' and give you money. Or they will say 'no' and not give you money.

This establishes a foundational mentality on which all efforts to raise money are then based: *You will get more money if you can get more people to say 'yes'.*

Determining if a fundraiser was successful or not then relies on two measurements.

1. Did you get enough money?
2. Did you get enough people to say 'yes'?

Did you get enough money? That's a fairly straightforward calculation. We needed this much and we got this much

One hospital celebrates that it was more than we needed!

Another hospital is thankful that it was enough.

Another hospital is devastated that it wasn't enough…

Success is determined by whether the money collected is enough or not enough. Simple.

The numbers get a little more tricky when we try to crunch human data. Math does not always provide us with intuitively clear answers regarding campaign success when it comes to the human side of things because it all depends on *what numbers you're working with* and *how you crunch them.*

To determine success when analyzing the people involved you now have two ways of calculating success:

1. Did we get a high enough *number* of people to say 'yes'?
2. Did we get a high enough *percentage* of people to say 'yes'?

For-profit tools marketed to non-profits use sales tactics that focus on these two factors. The tool will either help you increase your number of donors (ex. Pop-up website plugins to grab people's emails, phone and mailing lists for sale, web services to increase website traffic, search engine optimization services to get you better visibility on Google, etc) or increase your conversion/response rate (ex. Web payment portals to ease donating with the click of a button, sales training for your team, tools to make your event more engaging, products you can sell that are more enticing, etc).

Having been bombarded by sales message from the for-profit realm the non-profit organizations then buy into their tools and get to work. They work to increase their list of email contacts, phone numbers, and mailing addresses and attempt to increase face-to-face interaction through canvassing more houses, setting up shop in higher foot traffic locations, and attending more networking events. They work to find better products to sell, better events to run, better promotional items to distribute, and better tools for collecting money.

Let's say the end result is that last year they got 17 people to donate and this year they got 170 to donate. If you are basing fundraising success on the number of donors then these numbers definitely suggest you are heading in the right direction.

But if you're crunching percentage numbers you might change your tune. How many people did you have to approach to get those 170 donations? Did you approach 250 people and 170 gave you something? That's an amazing 68% response rate! Did you approach 3000 people to get those 170 donations? That's an abysmal response rate of less than 1%. The question is less about how many people you reached out to, but about how many of those people gave.

Because the percentage of response is a reflection of return on investment of energy and resources dedicated to asking I think the percentage is the better calculation to lean towards. If you print and mail brochures for 300 people and 17 make a donation, you might just get enough money back in donations to cover the costs of the brochures and postage! That's not a good return on the resources of time and money that you put into that endeavour.

Focusing on increasing your response percentages, therefore, seems like the wisest solution. But percentage calculations can still send people down a path of investing their resources unwisely if they are looking at the equation from the wrong side.

A non-profit organization running a fundraising campaign would likely be very encouraged by a 17% response rate to their efforts. If they sent out 100 letters asking for money and 17 people respond with a cheque, that's pretty good. If they stop 100 people on the street and 17 of those people give them money, that's a great response rate. And if 17% is great then 18% and higher would be even better! Every fundraising tool that I have come across to date has approached the percentage equation from this side. The side focused on the few who responded and raising that number as high as they can get it. But it's really hard to crack that 17% threshold. And here's the reason why.

I'd like to propose that the tools are looking at the pool of donors from the wrong end of the percentage equation. As a team builder, when I see that a non-profit got a 17% response from their request for support I don't see a high number. I see a horribly low one. Because what jumps off the page at me is that there was a failure to receive support from 83% of the donor community.

Failing to get a response from 83% of one's community is a big deal! The question for me becomes not about how to increase the number of donors who give, but about why that perfect number of 100% has dropped so low? From a team building perspective, I know that a 100% response rate when we ask for help is possible. Not just possible, but actually a reliable outcome we can depend on when we are connected to a strong support network.

So please allow me to share a team builder's perspective on fundraising, why its traditional practices are shooting people and organizations in the foot, and how a different perspective could open up whole new worlds of possibilities for you when it comes to meeting your needs as an individual or an organization.

I'll start with this thought. The majority of fundraising tools available today are not bad, in fact, many of them are quite valuable and high-quality. However, they will not help organizations crack the 17% response rate ceiling because of one fatal flaw. Fundraisers ask *individuals* for *funds*.

4

PEOPLE ARE WEIRD
IN TWO WAYS

We are no longer going to question *if* people want to give. We are no longer going to look at humans as individuals who are like vaults. There is no psychological pin combination we can devise to crack them open and get their money. Everyone is open all the time because there is a sociological phenomenon that we all compliment each other and that whoever you are, whatever you are trying to accomplish, everyone is open to giving to their connections in some way.

PEOPLE ARE WEIRD IN TWO WAYS

I feel sorry for anyone given the task of managing a fundraising campaign that requires them to go out and ask for money. The level of pressure on that individual is incredible. The very nature of the task has set them up for experiencing the unnecessary levels of stress associated with being asked to accomplish something that goes against human nature.

The majority of fundraising campaigns, and the support tools that I have come across which taught the organization to do things that way, do not work in tune with human nature or outright fly in the face of it. The problem is that they treat donors as *individuals* and focus primarily or solely on the *psychology* of giving.

Psychology is the scientific study of why human beings do the weird things they do inside their heads. It's the weird things you do as *you*. Think about it. The theories answer questions about why you prioritize things the way you do, why your thought processes developed the way they did, why you react to certain situations the way you do, etc. It's all about you, you, you. And fundraising tools consistently treat every donor as an individual whose psychology just needs to be understood well enough, or engaged or manipulated in just the right way, to get the person to open their wallet.

When fundraisers approach each person as though they are going to be willing to open their wallet and hand over money under some circumstance (the fundraiser just has to figure out what that circumstance is) this demonstrates that they have failed utterly to consider the *sociology* of the donor.

Sociology is the scientific study of why we do the weird things we do when we're *together*. It's the weird things you do when you're around other people. Think about it. The theories answer questions about why you are less likely to call 911 at an emergency scene if another person got there before you did, why you're likely to mirror other people's very bizarre behaviour in a social setting if everyone else is doing it, etc. It's all about us, us, us. And campaigns that treat donors as a *body of people* or a *community* rather than individuals are the ones that are going to get the best returns.

The reason that fundraising efforts tend to get a 17% return and max out around this number is not because they've only engaged 17% of their target donor audience, but because *they've tapped out 100% of their donor community whose primary way of giving is in the form of no-strings-attached money or 'funds'.* Many non-profit organizations who fundraise, even those who appear to be doing so successfully, are often only tapping into <u>one-sixth</u> (17%) of the resources available to them. One-sixth? Where did that number come from? Read on!

Funds are cash that can be diverted wherever your organization sees fit. The donor is being asked to give money that they ultimately have no idea what its use will be. Will it be used to buy pens or pay for a plane ticket? They have no idea! To ask for money without telling the person you're asking how you will use it is a pretty audacious maneuver. And non-profits do it *all the time*. For approximately 17% of the population, if you tell them that the money will be used to "help your child's school" or "support flood relief" that is enough. They will trust that you know what you are doing and that the money is in good hands to accomplish what you said it would accomplish. For 83% of people, that message does not click. They would be more than happy to support your cause. But not through funds. There are in fact six resource categories that donors are willing to give from at any time and money/funds is only one of them. Campaigns that have this narrow focus have difficulty cracking the 17% ceiling, and may not have percentage numbers anywhere near that high, if they're not sure how to tell the difference between their *contacts* and their *connections*.

Here's what I mean. Let's say an organization emails 300 people asking them for support. If they get 17 responses out of the 300 people they contacted and base their response rates on that number their results will look just terrible. That's less than 1%. But having someone's *contact* information doesn't mean you have a *connection* with them. If the organization instead knows they have established connections with 100 of those people and calculates the 17 out of that 100 that's a 17% response rate. Well done! (Diagram 1)

Now here's why the other 83% matters so much. Those other 83 *connections* would have given to you if you asked for help. It's what we do when we are genuinely connected to someone else. However, *you didn't ask for what they were willing to give.* There are 6 Key Resource Categories that human beings are willing to give from at any point in time, it just depends on who is standing in front of them and what they are asking for. Money in the form of funds is only one of those six categories. 1/6 (17%) of your connections will give you money because that is what they always would have done based on who you are and the particular request you made. 5/6 (83%) of your connections will never give you money based on who you are and the particular request you made. Money is not the resource category that resonated with them when you made the request that you did. That's where the perception that there is a yes/no equation at work comes from. If you ask for money then the people who give money will say yes.

If you ask for money then the people who give from other resource categories will say no!

DIAGRAM 1

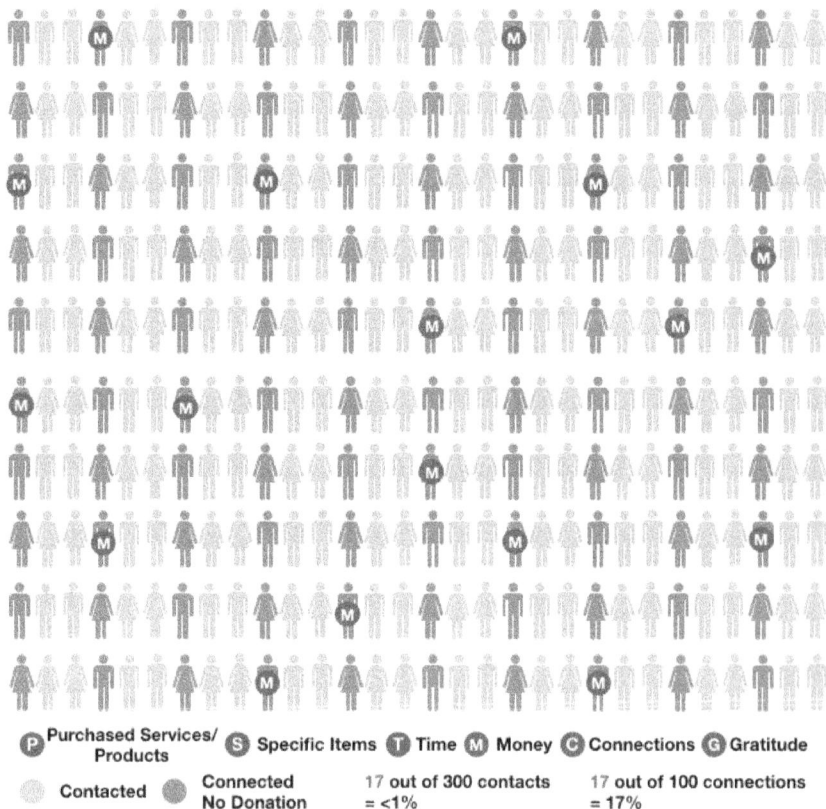

| P Purchased Services/Products | S Specific Items | T Time | M Money | C Connections | G Gratitude |

| | Contacted | ● | Connected No Donation | 17 out of 300 contacts = <1% | 17 out of 100 connections = 17% |

But if you ask for what they are willing to give, covering the bases of all The 6 Key Resource Categories, then *every one of your connections is willing to say yes.*

My hope with this book is to get you connecting with your donor community in such a way that when you ask for help, 100% of your connections give. Not just to meet your goals, but to help you exceed them beyond what you ever thought possible.

Here is step one to making that happen. You have to stop running fundraising campaigns. From here on out I am going to be referring to your *resource campaign*. It's not money that makes it possible for you or your organization to accomplish its mission, it is *resources*, and I want you to be swimming in them.

Here are The 6 Key Resource Categories we're going to be reaching out to your connections for:

THE 6 KEY RESOURCE CATEGORIES:

Purchased Services/Products ($)
I want something of value in return for my money

Specific Items ($)
I know exactly how my gifts are being used

Time ($)
I will volunteer to do a job or provide a skillset

Money ($)
I trust you'll do the right thing with no-strings-attached funds

Connections
I will help you with laser-focused networking

Gratitude
I will offer positive contributions and commitment

I'll highlight now that four of The 6 Key Resource Categories are in fact money ($). But only one of them is *funds*. If someone gives you something you needed so you don't have to pay for it, that's money still in your hands. If someone volunteers their time and skillset meaning you don't have to pay someone to do that job, that's money still in your hands. Someone purchasing the services or product your organization offers (and you better have one, we'll talk more about that later) is money coming in.

There is tons of opportunity to gather money during a resource campaign, but some of that money is going to be in disguise.

There's one more thing you need to know to really grasp why resource campaigning so powerfully resonates with your connections. A single person might lean strongly towards giving out of one category on a more regular basis, but when you look at the big picture of their lives they will have given from every category many times. Because every person in a community is going through a *constant flux of responding from different resource categories* depending on *who* is in front of them at the time and *what* they are asking for. It's the nature of our sociology. It's a weird thing we do when we're together in a community of any kind.

This means that multiple non-profits operating in the same community all have the opportunity to have their needs met in wonderfully creative ways. They're not all in competition with each other to get their community's limited amounts of money. Instead, they are connected together in a community filled with resources that will exchange hands based on expressed needs within that community.

I'll use myself as an individual example. When I come across an organization that says they can stop babies from dying, I will give them my money in a heartbeat. I always thought that the death of a newborn was a sad thing, but after having my son the idea of a parent losing their baby makes my heart seize up and my breath stop. No parent should ever have to go through that. I will happily give someone my money if they tell me they can make that stop. But if someone shows up at my door asking for money for the local animal shelter, there is no way I'm giving them money for that. It's not because I don't respect or support those who care for homeless and abused animals, it's just that I don't want to give them my money. But if they asked me for blankets I would grab every blanket in my home that I don't need and give it to them in a heartbeat. Of course, your dogs can have my blankets! I want them to be comfortable!

If someone you've connected with turns you down it's because you're asking for something from a category they are not interested in giving from. *But if you connect with them and cover all your bases they will always be willing to give you something from the category that resonates with them based on who you said you are and what you said you do* and the resources will start pouring in.

Now for the community perspective....

If you are an organization that prevents newborn mortality through health initiatives in impoverished countries and you connect with 100 people they will give you the following (Diagram 2):

DIAGRAM 2

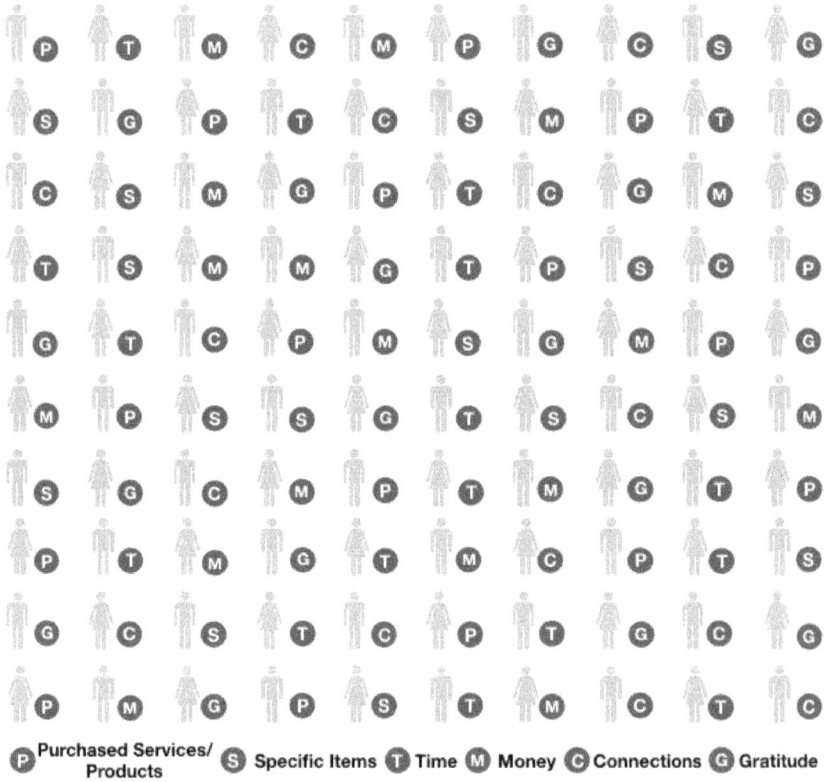

P Purchased Services/ Products S Specific Items T Time M Money C Connections G Gratitude

If you are an organization that rescues homeless and abused animals, providing them with healthcare and finding them loving homes, and you connect with those same 100 people they will give you the following (Diagram 3):

Resource campaigns tell people what you want to accomplish and what resources from The 6 Key Resource Categories you are looking for to help make that happen. Depending on who you are and what you are asking for the resource category they give from may change from one organization knocking on their door to another.

This phenomenon has sent many a fundraiser scurrying back to their drawing board wondering how the other guys got money out of a target donor, but they didn't! Newsflash, if you connected with a person and they didn't give you money they will probably never give you money because your organization and request don't click with them in that category. But they will give you other resources.

DIAGRAM 3

T	P	G	M	G	S	C	M	S	C
S	M	S	P	C	T	G	S	P	C
M	T	G	M	T	P	M	M	C	S
P	S	G	G	C	P	S	T	M	T
C	P	M	S	G	S	G	G	T	M
G	T	S	S	M	P	T	C	T	G
S	M	C	G	S	P	C	G	P	T
T	P	G	M	P	S	C	T	P	S
M	M	T	P	C	T	P	C	M	C
T	G	C	S	T	P	G	M	P	C

P Purchased Services/Products S Specific Items T Time M Money C Connections G Gratitude

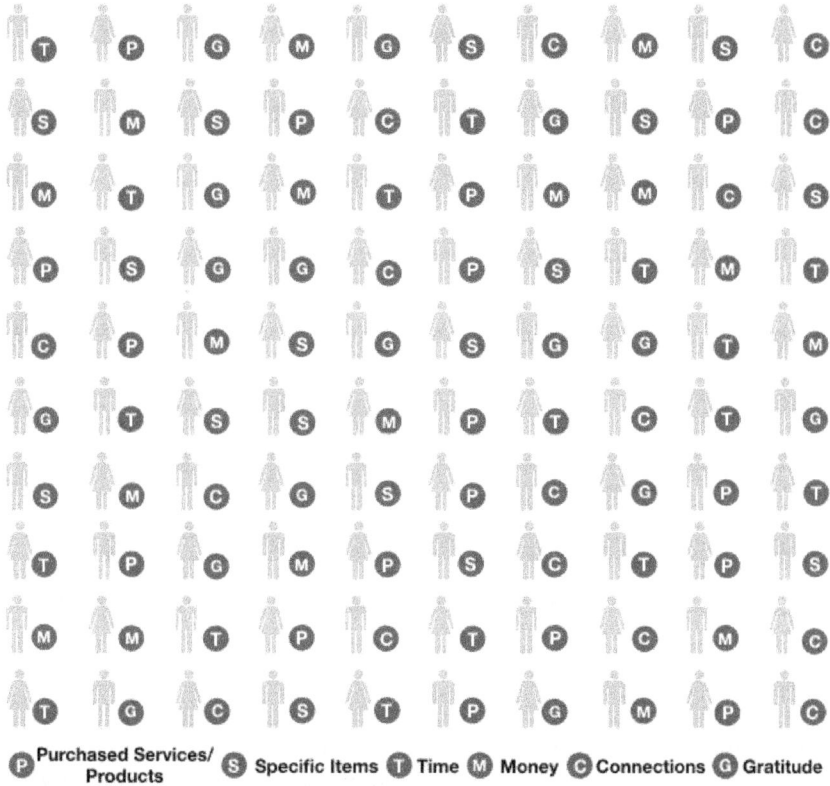

The amazing thing is that in the end, when you start seeing your donor community as a greater whole, it doesn't matter what category they give from because, as a whole, a group of people will ultimately provide what you need. And for anyone who wants to argue that it doesn't work that way because there's always that guy who hates your cause or is a complete miser and wouldn't give anything to save his life, then fine, let's factor him in.

There he is (Diagram 4).

DIAGRAM 4

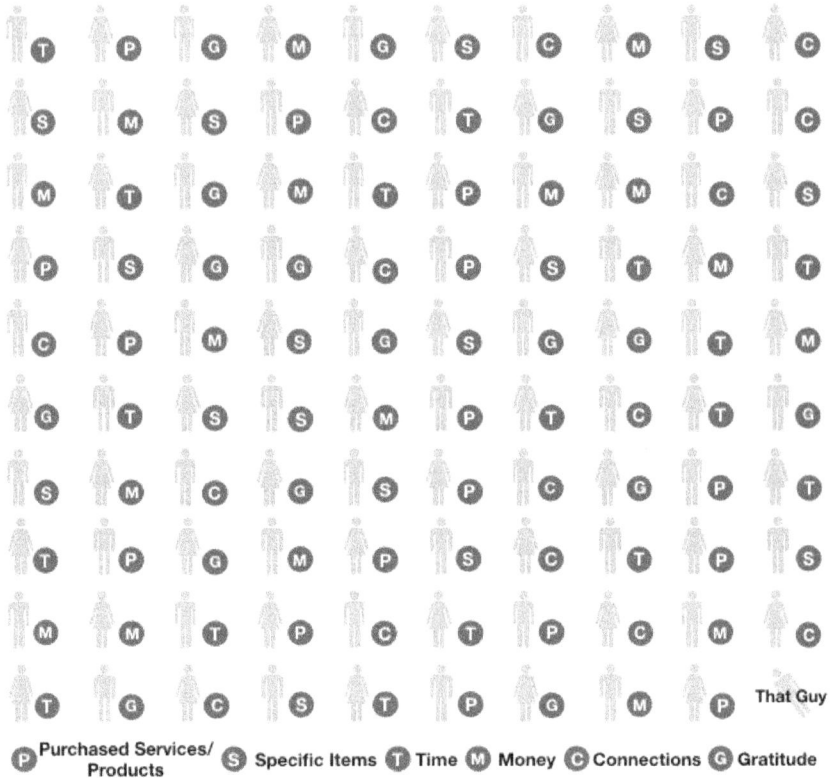

T	P	G	M	G	S	C	M	S	C
S	M	S	P	C	T	G	S	P	C
M	T	G	M	T	P	M	M	C	S
P	S	G	G	C	P	S	T	M	T
C	P	M	S	G	S	G	G	T	M
G	T	S	S	M	P	T	C	T	G
S	M	C	G	S	P	C	G	P	T
T	P	G	M	P	S	C	T	P	S
M	M	T	P	C	T	P	C	M	C
T	G	C	S	T	P	G	M	P	That Guy

P Purchased Services/ Products S Specific Items T Time M Money C Connections G Gratitude

You still seem to be doing alright.

For organizations looking at this chapter so far and thinking to themselves, "we're already doing all that", are you? Here are two good filter questions to help figure out if you are running fundraising campaigns or resource campaigns. First, when you send out an appeal, do you ask for *all* of your needs to be met with *every* appeal? Second, are your fundraising campaign manager, volunteer recruitment manager, inventory manager, program director, communications director, and events coordinator all the same person or all working as a close-knit team? If the answer to either question is no, you are either running fundraisers and everyone else is doing their thing as a separate initiative (and waiting for you to bring in the money so they can do it), or you are dabbling with resource campaigning and have room to take your efforts to a whole new level!

The transition to resource campaigning means you have to leave behind the idea that funds and volunteering are different things, or that the physical items you need to operate are different from the money you receive for paid services you provide. They're not. Okay, they are different, but they are all *resources*. And it is going to take a campaign manager with a broader focus or a team of people working closely together to be able to create a comprehensive, multi-layered resource campaign. It's with that broader focus that your organization will be able to better consider every member of the donor community and *how they want to give*.

We are no longer going to question *if* people want to give. We are no longer going to look at humans as individuals who are like vaults. There is no psychological pin combination we can devise to crack them open and get their money. Everyone is open all the time because there is a sociological phenomenon that we all compliment each other and that whoever you are, whatever you are trying to accomplish, everyone is open to giving to their connections in some way. It's just a case of identifying *how* they are willing to give and being conscientious about how you ask.

Before we can learn how to ask your donor community for resources in such a way that everyone gives something we first need to look at the approach that is not only failing to connect with but actively pushing away 83% of your audience. Let's make sure those issues don't carry over and plague your new endeavours.

A NOTE ON MATHEMATICAL PHENOMENA

The 80/20 rule is a mathematic phenomenon in which an inordinate number of things on this planet break themselves down into an 80/20 split. 20% of the population is contributing 80% of a country's volunteer hours. 80% of an organization's problems are being generated by 20% of its staff. 20% of an organization's products or services are generating 80% of the net income.

There are plenty of resources out there to help you learn more including how you can apply the rule to your organization and benefit from the insights. However, it is important to know that the 80/20 rule isn't perfect. Sometimes the number comes out 70/30 or 85/15. The main point is that there is a disproportionate weighting of cause and effect and it's worth harnessing the rule to make wise decisions moving forward.

Noting that the rule seems to have struck again in the 83/17 split we see created by fundraising, it is important to not get hung up on the numbers, looking for every group of 100 people to have 17 people who give this and 17 who give that… The main point is that there is generally equal distribution of people within any community who will be happy to help meet your needs and wants in various ways. For this reason it is worth harnessing the principles of resource campaigning and The 6 Key Resource Categories to make wise decisions moving forward.

5

HOW TO GET ELDERLY PEOPLE TO GIVE YOU THE FINGER

Campaigns of any kind create an environment and an experience. The environment might be online or at a golf club. The experience might be touring a website or attending a gala. Whatever the environment and experience, your donors will take away additional messages you didn't intend to communicate, but that shout louder than any individual thing you said or did.

HOW TO GET ELDERLY PEOPLE TO GIVE YOU THE FINGER

I mentioned earlier that there are numerous campaign resources that unintentionally point organizations in the wrong direction and I'll sum up the problem with their underlying message this way.

The inherent nature of *fund*raisers requires *money-based communications*. They also have a tendency to refer to building a strong 'donor base', a financial foundation on which you can build your organization and achieve your mission.

With the underlying mission of getting enough money and getting enough people to say yes, those raising funds are encouraged to do the following:

1. Make their list of contacts as long as possible.

2. See their list of contacts as people they have a connection to.

3. Treat that list of connections as made up of two categories, those who are excited about giving to your cause and those who are not excited about giving to your cause.

4. Move as many people from the not-excited category to the excited category as possible.

The word 'excitement' is important here because this is consistently what the fundraising tools aim for and communicate. Excite! Excite! Excite! Demonstrate to the donor your passion for your mission! Find a personal connection! Did they participate in your soccer camp? Highlight that donating will support current young athletes! Have they lost a loved one to disease? Highlight that you are working towards making sure no family ever experiences that kind of loss again. The idea is that if you can ignite their passion, even just a little bit, then you should be able to get some money out of them (Diagram 1).

DIAGRAM 1

Money-Based Communication Strategy To Create Strong Donor Base

Not excited about donating   Excited about donating

Excite!	Demonstrate passion for mission ➤	Money!
Excite!		Money!
Excite!	Find personal connection ➤	Money!

Contact information = Connection
Excitement = Lots of Money = Success

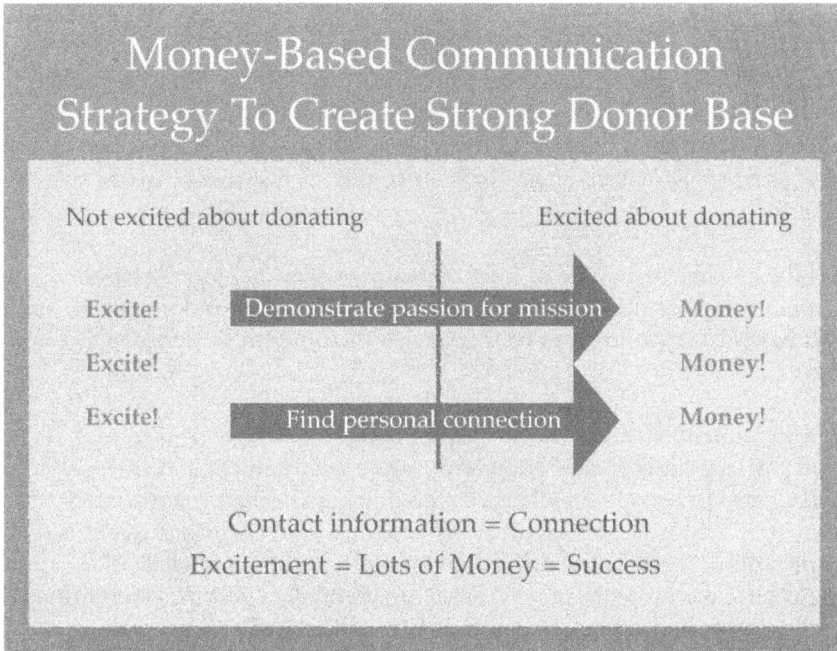

There is some sound psychology behind this method. *But only if you are talking to someone who is prone to giving funds based on who you are and what you said you do.* To anyone who gives from one of the other five resource categories, you are now talking to a brick wall. A brick wall that is getting increasingly annoyed. A brick wall that is now hanging up on you or ripping up your mail-out and skipping the recycling bin to toss it straight in the garbage. Further pursuit of this person to ask for funds is not going to weaken their defences. It will result in the wall being fortified and the person potentially firing back (ever been yelled at before someone hung up the phone on you or received a nasty email telling you to remove them from your mailing list?). This is the communication strategy that is triggering the classic yes/no response!

17% are willing to say yes. 83% have little or zero interest and say no. If someone says yes and you approach them again, their previous yes means there is usually an understanding of why you are back. They know their earlier support increased the likelihood of being asked again. And as long as the connection has been nurtured there is a chance that they'll support you with funds again. However, if they said no to your original request and you're back... Why? Why are you back at their door, on their phone, in their inbox, in their face? There is a defensiveness that can pop up because they said, "*No*". Keep trying to contact them after that point and you can kill connections, reverting that person back to 'contact' status or losing them entirely.

That's 83% of your connections whose 'no' can be triggered by a single appeal, and whose annoyance or outright anger can be triggered by any successive appeals. The overall message communicated by the experience is that *your 'no' is not important*. In what context is that message ever a good thing?

I want to make you aware of a few other messages that money-based communications shout loud and clear to the 83% of your donors who are not naturally responding to your appeal at the time with a desire to give you funds.

If you remember earlier, in the chapter about the history of this book, I told you that facilitation is about creating an environment and an experience through which people can take away so much more than you intended or thought possible. Campaigns of any kind create an environment and an experience. The environment might be online or at a golf club. The experience might be touring a website or attending a gala. Whatever the environment and experience, your donors will take away additional messages you didn't intend to communicate, but that shout louder than any individual thing you said or did. Here are some problematic ones.

1. YOU'RE A BIG FISH. YOU'RE A LITTLE FISH

Money-based communications are targeted primarily to who? People who have money! The more money a person has the more they generally have to resign themselves to having people banging on their door 24/7 asking to get their hands on some of it. It's like a lifelong fishing derby and they're the prized salmon everyone is after. And if we've bought into fundraising mentality then we congratulate the fundraisers who get something substantial out of them. You landed a big fish! How did you do it? What bait did you use? Then we try to mimic their success.

The problem is, just like using a shiny lure or tasty bait to get the big fish, we think we have to be shiny or have a tasty offer to get the donor and donation. Fundraising leads to an inordinate amount of *schmoozing*. Dressing in clothing that is both unnecessarily expensive and uncomfortable. Affecting an air of success and confidence. Steering conversations in order to deliver pre-planned words. Yuck. It's awful. So awful in fact that we've now identified it makes human beings sick. Literally physically and mentally ill. The stress of schmoozing causes physical and mental issues that can become debilitating. Both for the person putting on a suit like it's a costume and driving a car they are terrified to scratch in order to show that they can 'swim with the big fish', and for the person who is continually approached by fake people. It's not a nice feeling to have people show every sign of wanting to connect only to then switch gears to a pre-planned speech asking for money. We are human beings. Nobody wants to be a fish. And any campaign that creates this dynamic is shooting itself in the foot by insulting and harming the health of every person involved.

2. JOIN US! (BUT DON'T BECAUSE WE REALLY JUST WANT YOUR MONEY)

I love when I see the phrase "join us" in campaign materials that are only asking for money. What would that organization do if someone actually showed up at their office? I can just see the staff frozen in place like deer in the headlights while one person gets up the courage to approach the person and say, "Well, we don't actually need anyone right now…". Join us! But don't! No, really, please don't. We know what we're doing and how we want to do it and we don't really want you messing with that. But if you'd like to give us some money on the way out that would really help…

Campaigns that don't have an opportunity for people to step up and help in tangible ways, side-by-side, with their own two hands, are not only missing out on leveraging a powerful resource but are also lying to some degree if 'join us' is anywhere in their communications.

3. WHEN YOU DIE, CAN WE HAVE YOUR MONEY? WE DON'T MIND WAITING (BUT SOONER IS BETTER THAN LATER)

Ah, the legacy fund. This one takes a bit more explanation because as part of a resource campaign it can be a wonderful tool, but as part of a fundraising campaign, it's a really good way to get flipped the bird.

To start, we need to really grasp that asking people to consider donating to a legacy fund isn't asking them to give while they are living, it is asking them to give to you *when they are dead*. That changes the nature of the conversation right then and there.

We know that if we ask for funds only 17% of our connections will resonate with the message while the other 83% have a 'no' response triggered. If you ask for somebody's money when they die then 17% of your connections will be intrigued by the idea and be willing to give it consideration at the very least, even if they don't donate in that way. Being asked to leave something in their will is kind of a big deal, so even a large portion of your 17% funds donors are going to say no to this one. If a funds donor is willing to say no to this one because of how big a request is being made, any guess how the other 83% feel about having been asked?

The 'no' response can be more intense when it comes to legacy funds, triggering not just annoyance or anger, but outright disgust. If you trigger disgust then that's a broken relationship right then and there.

There is a higher probability of triggering a disgust response with a legacy fund if it is only used for fundraising purposes because it is a more audacious request that requires the donor to be dead in order to receive the gift. And if no other interest was demonstrated in *connecting* with the donor for other means *while they are still living* then the underlying message facilitated is, "When you die, can we have your money? We don't mind waiting. But sooner is better than later".

I'll provide a fictional scenario of a fundraiser whose environment and experience facilitate a nasty opportunity for broken relationships in order to provide clarity. A fundraising campaign, focused on gathering funds, has a legacy fund as one of its tools. It offers an annual Seniors Brunch for which invitations are sent to local retirement homes and assisted living apartment buildings. The crowd is a combination of people who attend because they have some connection to the organization and people who are attending because life has slowed down and the brunch is something to do. The annual event offers delicious food, hot tea and coffee, along with local entertainment. Inconspicuously placed at each table setting is an information package about the legacy fund. When the Master of Ceremonies for the event gets up to the microphone they give a ten-minute presentation about the great things their organization is up to and attempt to make personal connections with the crowd. This is followed with a thank you to everyone for coming and a reminder to people to take a look at the information packages available on their table as it is an opportunity for them to invest in the next generation. They can also consider leaving a donation in the box at the information desk. We'll look forward to seeing you at next year's brunch!

For simplicity, we're going to say within the crowd are 100 seniors who already had, or just made, a connection with the organization. Assuming all of them saw the information package and understood the premise behind it then here's what happened. 17 seniors were intrigued by the idea of the legacy fund. To leave a portion of their assets to an organization in their will is either an old or new idea, but since the organization asked, they're willing to consider giving some legacy money (as the organization calls it). Since it requires additional work contacting their lawyer the seniors may or may not get around to it. But they'll consider it and maybe even follow up on it. A few drop money into the donations box on the way out.

The other 83 seniors know that giving to this legacy fund is not for them. Some of them are annoyed that the idea was even raised. *I thought this was an invitation to a nice event, not a trick to get me in the door so you could ask me for money. That's disappointing.* Some of them are outright disgusted.

You tricked me. You didn't want to give me anything. Invitation to a free brunch? That was bait! You just wanted me in a chair so you could ask me for my money. When I'm dead! What is wrong with you?!? There wasn't a single young person in that room. You want that money sooner rather than later, don't you? You want me to invest in the next generation? I could mentor your next generation, or have given you other resources you need now, but no. You don't want that. You're just willing to put up with me long enough to ask me to put you in my will and then I can go home and get out of your hair until next year. This is disgusting, I'm out of here.

What's fascinating about human sociology is that if another organization were asking for the exact same thing (would you contribute to our legacy fund?) then one of those exact same horrified donors might happily add the organization to their will while one of those exact same happy donors would transform into being utterly horrified. It just depends on who is asking and what they are asking for. But that means *whoever is asking is always creating a 17/83 split* in the group of people they propose a legacy fund to if they are not asking for support in the form of all of The 6 Key Resource Categories. And the 83 will always say no, feel tricked, or be outright disgusted that you apparently are just waiting for them to die so you can get their money, reducing your chances of being able to rely on that relationship any further.

Environment and experience *matter!!!* I can not say it enough. Our journey of becoming more adept at resource campaigning receives a huge boost when we identify the old ways of fundraising that we're actively cutting ties with. We're leaving them behind so they don't poison our new efforts, souring the environments and experiences we create and facilitating unwanted messages. Our journey is forwards, deeper and deeper into the realm of resource campaigning where great things are waiting for us (Diagram 2).

DIAGRAM 2

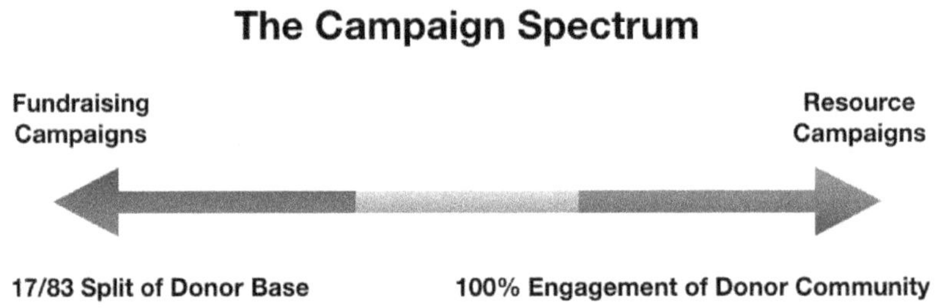

The Campaign Spectrum

Fundraising
Campaigns

Resource
Campaigns

17/83 Split of Donor Base   100% Engagement of Donor Community

So we wish a final farewell to the following.

Goodbye,

- Asking if we have enough *money*.
- Working to increase our *contacts*.
- Asking for support in the form of *funds*.
- *Schmoozing*.
- Trying to get people *excited about our cause*.
- Saying *"we'll accomplish our mission with your money"*
- Connecting with donors *to get money*.
- Being willing to *wait for people to die* so that we can benefit from their money.

We won't miss you. Onwards to better things!

Hello,

- Asking if we have enough *resources*.
- Working to increase our *connections*.
- Asking for support in the form of *The 6 Key Resource Categories*.
- Investing in genuine *relationships*.
- Trying to get people *connected with us*.
- Saying *"we'll accomplish the mission with our resources combined"*
- Connecting with donors *to work together*.
- Being willing to *engage with people today* so that we can benefit from each other's resources.

Let's get started.

6

DON'T DRIVE UP
THE
WHEELCHAIR RAMP

The remainder of this book is my attempt to start an industry-wide conversation about how we can adjust our current practices of asking for support and to give you some good intel. I hope to provide you with clear signs to send you in the right direction and set you up for success while the broader industry changes course.

My parents lent me their minivan for an epic Summer camping trip I was going on with a group of friends in my university years. It was an amazing week filled with adventures and random experiences which included the evening we decided to go see the presentation at the outdoor amphitheatre. We loaded into the van and with the campground's map in hand, we followed the directions and road markers until we had a problem. The road was heading up a hill and getting more and more narrow until finally, we came to a halt because any further and we'd be wedged between two trees. The roadmap and signs still said the amphitheatre was ahead, the pavement we were driving on hadn't changed, but the only option we had was to back up very slowly and very carefully to get back into wide open spaces and figure out what was wrong. We got far enough back down the hill to find a sign posted on a tree that was not visible from our direction of traffic and would have been sideways to us as we approached it. We had driven up the wheelchair ramp. That's a pretty horrible thing to do from the perspective of someone in a wheelchair (thank goodness no one was on the ramp at the time!!!). A minivan audaciously driving up the ramp, how dare they! But I didn't do it on purpose. I had a *map that said the road to where I was trying to go went this way.* I had *posted signs that confirmed I was on the right track.*

I don't think anyone telling organizations and individuals that they should be fundraising, and telling them how to do it, is trying to give their clients bad intel. The campground sure didn't intend to send me up the wheelchair ramp! The remainder of this book is my attempt to start an industry-wide conversation about how we can adjust our current practices of asking for support and to give you some good intel. I hope to provide you with clear signs to send you in the right direction and set you up for success while the broader industry changes course. I'd like to help you not drive up the wheelchair ramp.

We're going to shift our focus now to *relationship-based communications.* We know that people will give to us if we are connected to them so we're going to put our efforts into building, and being an active part of, a *donor community.*

With the underlying mission of gathering enough resources to achieve the mission together, those gathering resources would do well to focus on the following:

1. Make relationships with connections as rich as possible.
2. See the list of contacts as opportunities for new connections.

3. Treat the list of contacts as made up of two categories, those who you have a relationship with and those you do not have a relationship with.

4. Move people from the no-relationship category to the relationship category as opportunity genuinely presents itself.

The word 'connect' is important here because this is consistently what resource campaign tools aim for and communicate. Connect! Connect! Connect! Demonstrate to the donor your passion for your mission by just being you and talking about what you are genuinely interested in when the conversation goes in that direction! Find a personal connection by asking the other person what they are passionate about. Eventually, when we talk with people for long enough, we start to find commonalities whether related to our cause or not! (Seriously, sometimes people donate to an environmental group just because they found out the person asking them for help is also a huge fan of Led Zeppelin). The idea is that if you can connect, even just a little bit, then you'll be in a better position to work together and share the resources you have (Diagram 1).

DIAGRAM 1

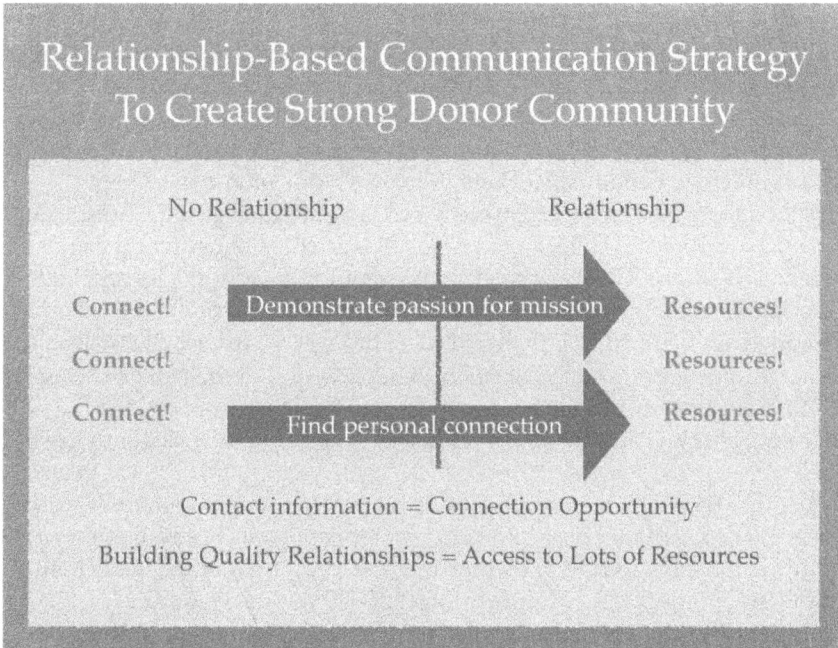

In the last chapter, I provided you with a fundraising scenario involving a legacy fund. I'd love to show you what a campaign resource scenario could look like in comparison.

A resource campaign, focused on gathering resources, has a legacy fund as one of its tools. It offers an annual Community Brunch for which invitations are mailed to known connections and homes in the area, and posters are put up at the local grocery store and library. The annual event offers delicious food, hot tea and coffee, along with local entertainment. Placed in the centre of each table is a summary of the organization's current needs. The list of needs includes looking for people to purchase tickets for an upcoming event they're offering, specific items they need to find, volunteer positions they're hoping to fill, funds to help with ongoing projects (people can make one-time donations, monthly donations, or give through the legacy fund), connections they are looking to make, and a reminder at the bottom to grab their free gift of locally bottled maple syrup at the information table on their way out! When the Master of Ceremonies for the event gets up to the microphone they simply thank everyone for coming, let them know if they'd like to connect or ask questions they can check in at the information table, and we'll look forward to the next time we see you!

Now for the breakdown. Let's say there are 100 people of all ages mixed into this crowd who already had, or just made, a connection with the organization. Of those present, 17 people were interested in giving money to support the organization. Thirteen chose to do so through a monetary gift at the information table where there was a donation box. Three grabbed forms that tell them more about how monthly giving works, and one person, a recent college grad who just started working full-time and opened their first RRSP last week, picks up a form about the legacy fund. The bank had only asked them to identify *people* that would be the beneficiaries of the RRSP if they died. They weren't informed they could leave their money to an *organization*! They plan to call the bank on Monday to find out how to add the organization as a beneficiary on the RRSP because what a great place for their money to go if they don't get to use it!

The other 83 people who attend are intrigued by other things they learned were needed, and they'd love to help out! Some people check in at the information table to find out where they can drop off needed items that they have. Others ask for more information about the volunteer opportunities. Some buy tickets for the upcoming paid event, some leave contact information for the connections the organization is looking for or say they'll contact the right person so they can follow up. And many people smile, wave, and say thank you as they walk past the information table on their way out. They had a really good time and think highly of the organization for throwing such a great event.

The two legacy fund scenarios represent the extreme opposite ends of the campaigning spectrum (Diagram 2).

DIAGRAM 2

The Campaign Spectrum

Fundraising
Campaigns

Resource
Campaigns

17/83 Split of Donor Base   **100% Engagement of Donor Community**

Many organizations are operating somewhere in between, but hopefully, the sample scenarios help to highlight that the more we invest in creating comprehensive resource campaigns the more our various efforts will positively pay off and the more we can trust that the tools we are using are helping to build our donor communities rather than break them down.

To create the best environments and experiences that foster the development and success of your resource campaigns you'll want to integrate the following foundational principles into every initiative as you go along. They will help to facilitate good things!

1. KNOW WHAT YOU NEED

Some organizations are going to be able to dive right into resource campaigning and immediately start seeing all the benefits because they already have a strong grasp of what resources they have, how they are being used, and what needs currently exist. For organizations who have been less diligent about knowing all the ins and outs of their resources, there might be some hard work necessary to help you properly get your resource campaigning feet under you.

Do you know exactly how much your organization has in assets and liabilities? Do you know what resources will need to be renewed, repaired or replaced within the next ten years? Do you know where the majority of your resources are coming in from? Do you know where the majority of your resources are being used? Do you know what part of your organization has the best returns? Do you know what part of your organization is leaking waste? If you don't know the answers to these questions you need to find out. First of all, so you can operate your organization responsibly. Any organization who says it will cost $100 to dig a well for an impoverished village is lying if that $100 does not result in a well being dug for an impoverished village. Know what it's costing you for administrative tools and salaries. Know how much money you need to set aside to cover upcoming costs and not just the initiatives you want to pursue today. Knowing what you need will shape what you ask for and how you word it and this can make or break donor relationships.

If you're feeling overwhelmed by the idea of how many records and documents and meetings you'll have to get through to get the answers, then gather a team or hire a professional. In a later chapter on transitional change, you'll also find lots of ways that you can start applying resource campaign strategies to your organization while you get the answers. You don't have to have the answers before you start. But you do need those answers in hand if you are going to get the most out of everything resource campaigning has to offer.

If you are an individual who is raising support for yourself or trying to gather the resources you need to thrive, knowing your needs will really help you get past the idea that you need *money*. Be honest and ask yourself, what do I need? Some things to take into consideration are food, clothing, shelter, money to pay necessary bills and fees (ex. Renewing your driver's license), money set aside for retirement (don't forget to think about the future!!!), and any needs you have specific to your work or cause that you are dedicated to.

When you know your needs and start resource campaigning it can make the difference between raising money to pay for rent or asking your donor community to provide a place for you to live. It can make the difference between saying you need money for groceries and asking your community for meals. It can make the difference between asking for money to buy clothes and asking for the clothing. Individuals who ask for money to get the things they know they need will generally be working much harder than those who know exactly what they need and can communicate that to others so their donor community can meet those needs.

You can ask for perks too. No one said you can only ask for the necessities when raising your own support or meeting your personal needs. Resource campaigning allows you to say up front that you're a coffee addict and function best with large amounts of caffeine in your system so you're hoping to get a nice espresso machine. It's a very real possibility that someone will give you one! Somewhere within your donor community, there may be a lonely machine sitting on the counter of someone who gave up caffeine because it gave them migraines and they'd love to regift it to someone who can give it a good home. Love to snowboard and that would help you relax and recharge after working hard? Ask for a snowboard! Love going to the movies to unwind? Ask for passes to the local theatre! Resource campaigning allows you to express both your needs and your wants so make a list and don't leave anything off!

A NOTE ON COMMUNICATION STRUCTURES

It is worth the time to double check and ensure that your organization makes it possible for every member of your team to express needs and wants that they see, not just managers. Can your janitor tell you their needs and wants so those things can be included in your resource campaign? How about your cafeteria staff? The new volunteer? If there is *a single person* who does not have the ability to submit their needs and wants, then it means you do not have the full picture and are missing out on an opportunity to add requests to your resource campaign. Take the time to ensure there are as few obstacles as possible, as few layers as possible, as little paperwork as possible between all of the members of your team who see a need or want and the person who can add that to the resource campaign.

2. HELP PEOPLE SEE YOUR BIG PICTURE

Have a place where people can go *at any time* to see what *all of your current needs* are. There is zero reason to not make resource campaigning a 24/7 initiative because of the existence of the internet. Wordpress.com lets you set up a website or blog. Facebook lets you set up free Facebook Pages. You might already have your own website or other online platform. Imagine a place where there was a permanent shopping list of all the things you need, want, and are willing to offer and that as a result, you had space to explain why you need or want something and to expand on the details if you're looking for something specific. Imagine being pleasantly surprised when you wake up one morning to find an email from someone you've never met offering you something you need. Imagine being encouraged when a package arrives in the mail that is one of the items you asked for, paid for and shipped by someone who saw your list.

Don't divide your list of needed and wanted resources out of fear it will look like you're asking for too much!!! As best you can, let people see the big picture so they can see all the different ways they can help! If you have people going door to door or trying to connect with people at events make sure they have physical copies of the shopping list or have ways to access it online (ex. Having a tablet that allows people to scroll through the needs you have posted online.). If you connect with someone, something will resonate with them and they will give! Because making a connection is so important here, remember to include a bio of who you are, what you're up to, and where possible provide updates so people who give can see the difference their donation made. This will also help build confidence for new donors to join in. To learn more about connecting, read on!

Note: For those organizations and individuals who do not have access to the internet because of lack of access or lack of money, having a written record that you can produce upon request will help you gather your resources more quickly. Do you have a public bulletin board you can post your current needs on? Do you have a piece of paper you can fold up and keep in your wallet at all times?

3. CONNECT! CONNECT! CONNECT!

Relationship-based communication strategies do not make the giant leaping assumption that having someone's contact information equals having connected with them. Or that people who walked past you (ex. Table set up in the front of a grocery store) were a missed opportunity.

Relationship-based communication sees a list of contacts or people who will walk past as an *opportunity* to connect. Having the ability to contact someone is not in and of itself proof that a connection has been made. Having someone walk towards you, see your sign, ask a question and keep walking is not in and of itself proof that a connection has been made.

Relationship-based communication breaks down contact lists or the crowd into two categories, those the organization does not have a relationship with and those they do have a relationship with. The goal is to move people from the first category to the second and the fortunate thing about switching to this communication strategy is that you're not totally starting from scratch. You can take your ability to demonstrate a passion for your mission and ability to find personal connections with you into this new model. They will help you start conversations! It's the goal of the conversation that has changed. Rather than trying to *Excite! Excite! Excite!* for the purpose of asking for money, you are now aiming to *Connect! Connect! Connect!* in order to share that you need *resources*.

Spending time to get to know the donor a bit better helps you to develop quality relationships. Relationships result in people being open to sharing their resources from one of The 6 Key Resource Categories depending on who you are. For a non-profit organization (or starving student/debt-buried adult/surviving senior) this means the ability to gather and make use of a lot of resources!

Remember how I shared earlier that many organization's donor statistics are skewed because they are looking at the number of people who donated out of the number of people they contacted or who walked past them? Look the next time you pass a donation table and see if there is someone standing or sitting who seems to be more focused on scanning the crowd and is fidgeting with an object in one hand. It's not a fidget cube, it's a counter. They are clicking a button for every person who walks past in order to calculate at the end of the fundraiser how many people they had the opportunity to access and how many they actually got something from. This practice of looking at the number of contacts or people who walked past completely messes up your numbers because contacting and connecting are *not the same thing* and it makes your numbers look just awful. Trust me, if you're asking for money you're getting donations from 17% of the people you connected with. Leave the counter at home because once you switch to resource campaigning it becomes completely useless. If you *connect* with someone you will always get a 100% return.

I want to be very clear that I am not trying to demonize the idea of asking for money. Giving up fundraising doesn't mean that you have to stop asking for funds. If you didn't ask for funds then 17% of your donor community would feel at a loss for how to contribute! There will always be people who want to give you their money. But resource campaigning is going to take you to a whole new level of having your needs met!

4. COVER ALL YOUR BASES (ie. THE 6 KEY RESOURCE CATEGORIES)

Your previous door-to-door fundraising efforts might previously have sounded like this:

Hi! My name is Lindsay and I'm with Save the Ferrets. We're a non-profit organization that rescues abandoned ferrets and finds them new loving homes. We're wondering if you would be interested in supporting our work with a financial contribution?

Having experienced the transforming power of becoming a resource campaign, it would then sound more like this:

Hi! My name is Lindsay and I'm with Save the Ferrets. We're a non-profit organization that rescues abandoned ferrets and finds them new loving homes. We're currently in need of some resources and I'm wondering if I could have 30 seconds of your time to share some of the things we are looking for. (No? Skip to the wrap-up. Yes? Continue!)

Great! Money always helps, but we're also looking for two more volunteers to help cuddle the ferrets and help them get exercise. We're looking to get our hands on enough kennels, food dishes, and water bowls so that we can take in three more ferrets. We also have ferret birthday parties that we offer for children ages 5-10 and we're trying to find families who would love to give their child a fun and furry birthday while learning about the animals. Do you have any interest in any of the things I've mentioned so far or know someone else who might be?

[Hear the response of the person and respond accordingly. At the end of the conversation finish with one of these two wrap-ups]. Before I go, I just asked you to help us, is there anything we can do to help you? OR Before I go I just wanted to let you know that we're giving back to the community with our annual Valentine's Day delivery ferrets. Our team will be delivering 50 valentines cards around the city with the help of our rescue ferrets who will hand the card over to the intended person. It adds some random fun to the day and we're not asking for anything in return. If you'd like one of our ferrets to deliver a card to your valentine you can go to this website to fill out the form.

[For more conversation starter templates please see Appendix C.]

If you don't have anything coming up where you are giving back to your community then simply asking the person you are speaking with if there is any way you can help them covers the base of asking for their gratitude. It might feel like a dangerous blank check to hand someone. They could respond with anything! But the reality is that most people will say they don't have anything they can think of and they will still sincerely appreciate that you asked. Those that do ask for help will usually be looking for help in the form of more information (What the heck is a ferret?). And for the rare random requests for help (Since you asked, can you get my Christmas decorations down from the top shelf for me? I can't reach them) you can respond using your discretion.

Gratitude is the least tangible of The 6 Key Resource Categories and I promise I'll expand on it further when we get to that chapter. For now, just know that you are building goodwill and do not ever underestimate the wonderful things that can happen when someone is just grateful that you are a part of their community and world.

If you remember to cover multiple bases in your initial interaction, hitting up as many resource categories as you reasonably can in your introduction without blabbing on forever, then you're probably going to walk away at the end of the day with the following. Cash in hand, three email addresses to give to the volunteer coordinator to follow up with more details, a plastic bag with a food bowl in it that one family didn't need anymore, a phone number so the events coordinator can follow up and book a birthday party, a promise to call a friend who just put two kennels up on Kijiji last week to see if she might be willing to donate them instead, and the gratitude of several people who actually appreciate this random encounter and having learned that there are people in the neighbourhood who are passionate about helping these little furry creatures.

In order to truly make the transition from fundraising to resource campaigning, you will have to grab ahold of the following concept.

Covering all of your bases does not mean rotating between what tools you use to reach as many donors as possible. It means that no matter what tool you are using, at any given time, you are always prepared with a list of your current needs so that you can ask for something from each of The 6 Key Resource Categories.

Always know as much about your needs as possible. Always have a current list of those needs. Always cover all of The 6 Key Resources Categories when you share what you are looking for in any donor interaction!

5. SHARE YOUR TRIUMPHS AND CHALLENGES

In the immortal words of the Dread Pirate Roberts, "Life is pain, Highness. Anyone who says differently is selling something." First of all, if you didn't know that was from The Princess Bride, drop everything and go watch the movie. I'll wait. Second, if your communications with donors make it sound like your organization has no problems, people consciously or subconsciously feel like you're selling something instead of trying to connect with them, and they don't like it. Newsletters that only say what's going well are junk mail because the recipients know it's not accurate. Newsletters that share what's going well and what current challenges exist or are coming up are *communications* and donors respond much more positively to receiving these. This doesn't mean you have to be melodramatic or find problems so that your newsletters can be 'balanced'. You don't need to have equal pain to balance out the awesomeness that you're experiencing. Sharing triumphs and challenges just means being honest and transparent about how life is going. If things are great then tell people that. If things are not great you can say that too.

The bigger picture of your communications will add up to the greater whole of life with its ups and downs and people enjoy following that kind of plot. People don't watch tv shows and movies where everything goes perfectly all the time. To have a plot there needs to be conflict, challenge, a problem to solve. That is what engages people!!!

Don't make the mistake of thinking you always have to put your best foot forward to get more donors. That's terrible advice from the fundraising mentality of Excite! Excite! Excite! You can't tell your donors you had ten people quit over a dispute about HR policies! No one will get excited about that! They'll pull away and stop giving their money!

Or...

If you share that you have recently lost ten team members over an HR policy dispute and that while you are reviewing the HR policy in order to constructively move forward you need volunteers to provide help, this can make sure all your bases are covered during the transition. By the way, if you also say you have ten positions that need to be filled and ask your community to help you connect with good candidates you might find replacements faster than you'd think. Resource campaign mentality allows for transparency and genuine expression of needs because reaching out doesn't break connections, it builds them. Reaching out is how we connect in the first place. Don't hold your bad cards to your chest. It's okay to share the good things and the bad.

6. ASK EVERYONE

Depending on the nature of your organization, your cause, and the number of resources you need it's possible that you've been steering clear of certain neighbourhoods. Because what kind of person goes to the impoverished district and starts asking for things? They won't be able to give anything, right? Wrong. It would have been a problem if you'd been doing a fundraiser and walked up to homeless people asking them for money. But you're resource campaigning and everyone has resources of some kind. Remember that resource campaigning isn't asking *individuals* to support you through giving resources but is instead asking a *community* to support you. And the general rule with communities is that there is always enough to go around when you ask around and have both a give and receive mentality. *You can ask anyone for support because everyone in your community has equal ability to ask you for support too.*

The world is a big place so of course there will be stark contrasts. In some communities, there will be people willing to share the BMW parked in their driveway because their son got a new one for his birthday and doesn't drive this one anymore. In other communities, there will be families willing to share two of the four turnips they have left so another family lives one more day. I don't know where you're living, operating, or serving so the main principle I want you to take away is that it's okay to let anyone and everyone know what your needs and wants are no matter how much they appear to have or not have on the surface. A homeless man might be willing in a heartbeat to volunteer his time (and would be doubly grateful for access to the volunteer coffee and snack station). A family who is suffering trying to care for their son who is dying from cancer might have their spirits lifted when they see how happy their son is gifting his bike to another child who could use it. To state your needs and wants and ask people if they can help is not the same as walking up to someone and asking them to give you something specific that they're not ready to give. You're simply sharing your needs and creating an opportunity to give and it's a shame to take that opportunity away from people because we've made the wrong assumption that they have nothing to offer.

Give people the opportunity to give, and remember that you are part of the same community and therefore have equal opportunity to give to others yourself. Perhaps in connecting with people, you learn that the homeless man needs new shoelaces because his broke and his shoes keep falling off, or a family has been so focused on caring for their dying son that they haven't mowed their lawn for weeks. Giving up your laces and coming back two days later to mow the lawn is a great way of saying "we're all in this together." Resource campaigning acknowledges that we belong to communities of various sizes, that living in a community has both a give and receive aspect, and that this give and receive is healthy. It's okay to ask everyone.

Knowing that there is no reason to target or avoid certain neighbourhoods might also change how you reach out to people. Are you relying on website traffic, mail-out campaigns, social media, foot traffic, door-to-door campaigning, or other tactics? Do your current tactics focus on trying to connect with certain people and not others? If you're considering connecting with a new group that you had previously overlooked or avoided does that mean you need to change your tools to better reach them? Have fun exploring the possibilities.

7. COMMUNICATE CLEARLY HOW THE CAMPAIGN IS GOING

More is better, right? Wrong! So. Incredibly. Wrong. The concept is so prevalent because you find it woven throughout almost all fundraising support materials and campaign strategy resources. We're getting rid of fundraising mentalities and that means the concept of "more is better" has to go with it!

First of all, the "more is better" mindset allows a lot of opportunity for organizations to fall into irresponsible practices. Made impulse purchases that were a waste of resources? No worries, there's plenty in the bank right now. Not sure exactly how much you spent this quarter? No worries, there's plenty of padding to absorb some overspending. Not sure how much the new initiative is going to cost to maintain? All good, the team who gathers resources for us is really good and will get us what we need...

If you've been operating on the "more is better" principle there is a high likelihood that several things have been going very wrong within your organization and now is a great opportunity to clean house and get organized. How can you communicate to your donors how your campaign is going and how the resources are being used if you have no idea? Donor relationships are built and maintained on a foundation of trust. The more you can demonstrate you are trustworthy through accurate communication of how their donations are being used (ex. e-newsletter, AGM reports, website updates, social media posts, etc) the more likely you are to keep them as an ongoing donor.

Whether you've reached your goal or not will also impact a donor's decision to give, as well as *how they feel about you and the donation they gave you at the end of the campaign.* I remember watching a campaign play out for a building fund. A large amount of money was needed to pay the contractors hired to complete some repairs and updates to the organization's facilities, in addition to other resource needs, and the communications went out each week with appeals for people to give. The message interpreted by the donors from these emails was that the deadline was looming and the goal hadn't been reached yet so people continued to find ways to channel resources in the organization's direction. It turned out that wasn't the case at all. The goal had been reached a long time ago. When the leaders of the organization did a grand reveal, proudly showing how successful the campaign had been and how many surplus resources had been gathered which could now be used towards other initiatives the response from the community was less than positive. Some donors were angry. They had been happy to give and now just felt tricked. An official apology was issued with promises to communicate more clearly in the future, and this helped to soothe the situation somewhat, but damage to trust had occurred and that had farther-reaching consequences.

Please, when you ask for resources, do your best to stay on top of how the campaign is doing and be able to tell the people you connect with how much further you have to go, when the deadline is, and be honest if you've met your original goal. If you've already got what you asked for and the deadline hasn't arrived yet you can always create a 'stretch goal'. This means you can say you met your goal so you set a higher bar and are now trying to reach that. Or communicate that the additional resources will help you complete projects now that you originally thought would have to wait. Being able to tell donors that additional resources will now shave years off the launch date of an initiative is always exciting.

In the end just please don't make it sound like you are desperately trying to reach a goal that you met last Friday. Donors might be happy to give at the time, but if news gets back to them that they were duped, remember that broken relationships have a cost.

8. SHARE ALL OF YOUR NEEDS AND ALWAYS BE AVAILABLE TO RECEIVE, BUT DO NOT ALWAYS *ASK*

Fundraising literature has set the standard for making every communication about asking. Whether overt or subtle, there is always an *ask* included somewhere. Even people who are happy to give to you will get fed up if they are *asked* too often and they can *disconnect* from you. To be asked anything places a drain of some kind on our internal emotional resources. Just think of how many times a child needs to ask their parents 'why' before the parent snaps. Everyone has a breaking point. Please stop *asking*. But it's okay to continue regularly *sharing*.

For some reason sharing a need does not seem to place the same emotional strain on our internal resources that asking for a need to be met does. So review your communications schedule carefully. When do you reach out to communicate with your donor community? Do you have daily social media shout-outs? Weekly e-newsletters? Monthly mail-outs? Quarterly updates? Annual reports? Every communication you have with your donor community is an opportunity to *share* your current events and/or current needs. It is okay to keep people regularly updated regarding what you are looking for and where those resources can be sent if someone wants to give them. However, you need to choose very carefully a small number of times when you will very specifically *ask* or *appeal* for those needs to be met.

You'll want to make sure that times of asking are spread out and that they have periods of time in between where you've *shared* what life looks like right now and what your current needs are (Here's where we are. Here's what we're up to. Here's what we need. That is all. Carry on.) without *asking* for a darn thing.

Here are two examples to provide some clarity.

Sharing: Hi, Everybody! It's been a busy month of preparation and we're gearing up for our program launch next week! Just to let you know, we have three more spaces for people to register, are still trying to find a volunteer to provide weekend kitchen support, and are hoping to find one more guest speaker for the last week of the program who could provide inspiration and encouragement to our program grads. Our address and contact information are below if you'd like to get in touch. Cheers!

Asking: Hi, Everybody! It's been a busy month of preparation and we're gearing up for our program launch next week! We have three more spaces for people to register, are still trying to find a volunteer to provide weekend kitchen support, and are hoping to find one more guest speaker for the last week of the program who could provide inspiration and encouragement to our program grads. *Would you consider supporting our program by meeting one of these needs?* Our address and contact information are below if you'd like to get in touch. Cheers!

The addition of a single question has changed the tone of the communication and potentially the amount of emotional drain your donor community feels when reading it. When you make an appeal, ask for *everything* you need. But remember that you don't always have to appeal. You can share rather than ask and still have your needs met! The classic 'call-to-action' is a make-or-break moment when many donors decide whether to remain connected or ask you to remove their contact information from your records. Be sure to focus on connecting first and you're more likely to see a positive response and ongoing engagement when you do ask for action.

* * *

Because so much of our ability to engage in successful resource campaigning relies on our ability to connect and the health of our relationships there is one more topic we need to discuss before we can really dig into The 6 Key Resource Categories themselves. That topic is responsibility and accountability in regards to resources.

Poor responsibility and accountability in managing resources places intense strain on relationships and spending some time learning how to recognize and heal this relationship-eroding disease is one of the best investments you can make. Let's take a look now.

7

RESOURCE RESPONSABILITY & ACCOUNTABILITY

If you are going to connect with those who have the highest standards for earning their trust then you have to grasp this concept: To just ask people for resources without contributing anything in order to maintain your existence is disgusting to them. Those with the highest standards regarding resource responsibility and accountability consistently demonstrate a belief that to exist is your responsibility and that gifts of resources are only to help you reach further.

Individuals and organizations who can demonstrate financial responsibility and accountability are going to be the most successful at resource campaigning, no questions asked. The reason for it is that resource campaigning is relationship-based and relationships build their foundations on trust.

Trust in this case is built on the clear and honest communication of:

1. How resources are *going to be* used.
2. How resources *were* used.

Knowing how resources are going to be used requires planning ahead and crunching the numbers. Any accountant can tell you that 'more is better' is a terrible financial strategy. Knowing your numbers so you can be absolutely sure you've met your targets allows you to celebrate when you have gone above that number. Gathering 'more' without even knowing how much is 'enough' is a dangerous game to play.

Knowing how resources are going to be used also requires taking into consideration the bigger picture. Organizations break trust time and time again when they tell donors their $100 will help send a child to school for a year only to have donors learn through an audit that the organization devotes a large portion of that money to administrative expenses. Planning ahead means you know how much you need for administration and you know how much you need to send a child to school so you can communicate that clearly to donors. Donors will develop more trust with organizations who can say they need $75 to help the child and $25 to cover the administrative costs associated with helping them than with those who lump the $100 together which can make a donor feel tricked later.

Reporting clearly how resources were used after the fact then goes on to show donors that you fulfilled your word. Anyone comparing a before and after document would be able to see that things went where they were supposed to which deepens trust and increases the likelihood of that donor relationship continuing.

When it comes to reporting, organizations can easily fall into the due-diligence trap, only providing the mandatory reports that allow them to remain a non-profit in good standing. While this might meet basic government requirements, it doesn't open up a lot of opportunity with donors.

There aren't perfectly clear definitions of what resource responsibility and accountability mean. Everyone's take on the concepts is different in some way, but I can tell you this. The higher you raise the bar for your standards of resource responsibility and accountability the more you will exponentially increase the number of donors you have the ability to connect with and remain connected to. The lower you drop the bar for your standards of resource responsibility and accountability the more you will exponentially cut ties with donors and break off relationships. *The results are not proportionate.* Lower responsibility and accountability will close more doors to you than you ever thought possible. Higher responsibility and accountability will open more doors than you imagined (Diagram 1).

DIAGRAM 1

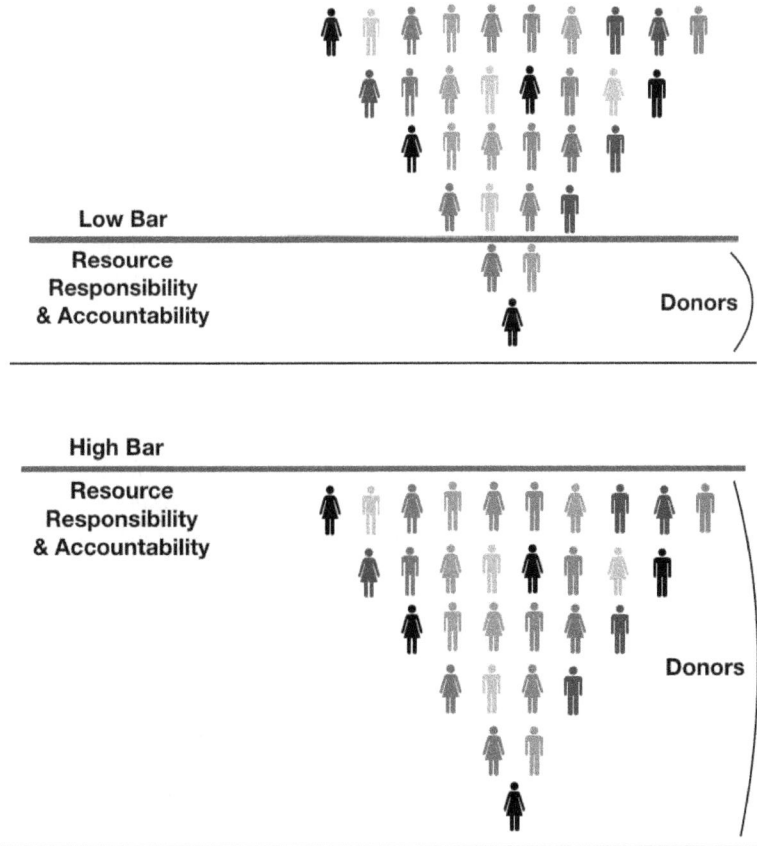

Keeping the bar high is so incredibly worth the effort!

Therefore, I am not going to provide you with low or medium bar recommendations. I want the best for you so I'm going to point you in the direction of some principles that will demonstrate high standards and open up the most opportunity to you.

If you're trying to figure out where you stand, where your bar rests and how many donors have been opened up to you, this guiding principle will help you know if you've cracked the top tiers or not.

Have you taken responsibility for your existence?

If you are going to connect with those who have the highest standards and earn their trust then you have to grasp this concept: *To just ask people for resources without contributing anything in order to maintain your existence is disgusting to them.* Those with the highest standards regarding resource responsibility and accountability consistently demonstrate a belief that to exist is your responsibility and that *gifts* of resources are only to help you *reach further.* They are not opposed to giving people resources. On the contrary, this tier of donors contains some incredibly generous givers. They are far from stingy. But they have to know that you are earning your ability to keep your doors open through smart and sustainable practices and that any time you ask for more it's because you're trying to expand your reach.

Human synergy is a beautiful thing and when you look at how we all play off of each other and bring balance to each other, it's a good thing these members of our community think the way they do. They help to bring greater accountability to organizations because they ask the hard questions and are less afraid to call something what it is. Did your organization spend money on something wasteful? They'll point it out. Did your organization take on a resource that had longer-term financial consequences that weren't considered and now you're in over your head with debt? They'll point out that the decision was foolish, ask you what you learned and what you're doing to responsibly get out of the situation.

They don't mind watching you squirm and they're definitely not going to bail you out of the consequences that are the result of your poor decisions (fundraisers to get out of debt make these guys *livid).* You're going to have to swim. But if you can demonstrate that you're on course for moving forward and that you're not going to swim head first into a debt whirlpool that you'll circle for eons, they'll canoe along beside you and cheer you on. If you can demonstrate that you are not going to swim back into the same undertow that got you in trouble in the first place and are charting a wise course for smooth water, then they'll be willing to give you the food and water you need to keep swimming.

If you cross paths with someone who starts asking a lot of uncomfortable questions or who wants to discuss concerns they have with your resource practices, don't write them off as difficult people who aren't interested in supporting you. They are interested in giving. The fact that they are still talking with you is a sign they are still interested in giving. If they had zero interest in a relationship they would end the conversation. The ongoing questions and discussion suggest they are instead searching for ways to build trust by getting the information they need to know you are trustworthy. If they are a previous donor whose trust was broken they may be sussing out if you understand what went wrong and if you're worth trying to trust again because you are now moving in a better direction. That conversation is not a waste of your time! It's helping to remove distrust or heal broken trust and individuals and organizations willing to invest in that process will see the returns in the long-run.

As part of creating a resource campaign with a high bar for resource responsibility and accountability, I *strongly* recommend investing the time and effort needed into answering these two questions:

1. WHAT IS THE BARE BONES STRUCTURE OF OUR ORGANIZATION?

In other words, what do we need in order to simply *exist*? Put your organization in a ten-year starvation scenario where there will be *zero gifts*. What would your organization need in order to continue existing through that ten years or else the organization would simply cease to exist? What would you prioritize devoting resources to if only the tiniest of scraps were available for you to work with and those scraps were resources you had to *earn*? This exercise helps you to do three things.

- It helps you to identify the difference between existence and reaching further.

- It helps you to plan ahead because there are many things that will break or need to be replaced or renewed in that time period that you'll want to be prepared for so you don't go under.

- It helps to identify if you are already carrying some unnecessary bulk. If your organization is wasting money sustaining something that is weighing you down instead of helping you take strides forward then that's a good thing to catch and deal with as soon as possible.

2. HOW MUCH DOES IT COST TO KEEP THAT BARE BONES STRUCTURE ALIVE?

No guesses allowed. You need a number. Without a number in hand, you automatically have your resource responsibility bar drop towards the bottom. You are either using your donors' gifts to reach further or you're not. It is absolutely irresponsible to tell donors a gift will help you achieve your mission if it's really going towards just keeping the lights on. So how much is needed to keep your bare bones alive? When you know that you will know exactly what the difference is between maintaining your existence and what is reaching further. You can now tell donors with confidence that their gifts are truly furthering your mission! And if you discover that your organization is, in fact, using money that was supposed to be used for your mission to pay for your rental space then you can start to fix the problem.

Taking ownership of your existence has everything to do with how you are *earning* your way. I want to highlight right now that a person's inherent value as a human being is not determined by what they earn. Your personal value will never change. The value of a group of human beings gathered together to take on a challenge together do not ever have their value determined by what they are able to collectively earn. So please do not make that connection. Instead, what I'm asking you to focus on is the need to *constructively contribute*. Around the globe, there are cultures with an intense focus on money and there are cultures where money is just not a thing. In both contexts there is a sense that individuals must each contribute in some way to their society, otherwise, they are lumps. They are taking up space. Even worse, they may be a drain on the community's resources. Everyone needs to contribute in some way.

In contexts where money is a strong part of the culture, it is wise to focus your efforts on earning your existence financially. This communicates to a larger percentage of people also operating in that cultural context that you are earning your way. To both gather resources, while communicating that you are earning your way, your efforts will be best invested in focusing first on Purchased Services/Products so that your donors can exchange money for something of value to them. I have come across camps able to sustain their existence through camp and retreat fees, and it is further donations that let them offer camping for free to so many others. I encountered a wonderful employment program with zero reliance on grants because they operate a coffee shop and cleaning service where their program participants gain workplace experience by operating these two businesses. Taking responsibility for your existence is possible! No matter who you are there is absolutely opportunity for you to earn what is needed to maintain your existence so that, come what may, you will still be standing! The chapter on Purchased Services/Products will tell you how!

In contexts where money is not really a thing because the culture does not rely on currency or you are in a region where no one has any, it is wise to focus your efforts on earning your existence through useful contributions. To both gather resources, while communicating that you are earning your way, your efforts will be best invested in focusing on Gratitude so that your donors can see that you are not a drain, but instead an active contributor to your community.

Here are some additional guiding principles for keeping your resource responsibility and accountability bar high.

1. BE TRANSPARENT

It can be tempting to try and hide flaws and mistakes. Nobody likes to admit they messed up. Even when we're doing well we know that opening up still exposes us to scrutiny and makes it possible for someone to point out that we could be doing better. For this reason, many individuals and organizations only release information they are legally required to provide. My encouragement to you is to throw the doors wide open.

In our age of the world being tied together by the internet, I've read some incredible stories of organizations making documents available that were otherwise considered private property and the outcomes they experienced were phenomenal. I read the story of a mining company unable to find gold who published all of their research and records of attempts to date, offering a reward to anyone who could help them find more deposits because they were stumped. People from a range of backgrounds, many that had nothing to do with mining, got in touch sharing insight from their realm of expertise and voila! Gold galore! I've read accounts of police departments releasing details of cold cases then having someone from another part of the country contact them to say they'd solved the mystery!

When you share the legally required financial spreadsheet at an AGM let's be real. The people looking at the sheet have no idea what it actually means. "Administrative Expenses". What does that mean? What was included on that line? Depreciation? How did you come to that number? What has been depreciating? How was the depreciation of that item calculated?

The more information you can provide, the better. If you can publish a spreadsheet that shows every vendor, dates of purchases, total costs, how much of the purchase price was taxes, etc you communicate to your donors that you are being transparent. That you are open to scrutiny, that you are willing to reveal your triumphs and your flaws, and that you are willing to accept their support in making things better.

If you post *everything* not only does this increase your internal accountability (your staff will think twice about wasteful spending if they know the receipt will be publicly published), but it also increases your external support. Vague resource reporting means you are relying entirely on your internal financial department and managers to catch mistakes. If you're an individual raising support then you might be the only person double-checking your figures. *Detailed* resource reports, reports that include *everything*, can mean that people go digging into your numbers, people you never thought would have shown interest. And yet they can get back to you with suggestions and help that make a world of difference.

Someone might see how much you're spending on electricity and offer to donate solar panels. Someone might see how much you're spending on healthcare supplies and be able to direct you to another vendor. Someone might see that depreciation was calculated incorrectly on a major item which means you're not in as good standing as you thought you were and action needs to be taken to fix that. Whether helping you tweak things to make them better or steering you away from the rocks, we live in an age where having more eyes looking at our details can be a good thing, not a curse.

Note: Before publishing resource reports, depending on the level of detail you have chosen to share, please review and make sure you have not included personal information that could result in identity theft. Where certain information could lead to abuse of your resources it is wise to keep that information private.

2. WHEN NEEDED, CONFESS RATHER THAN BEING EXPOSED

For anyone who feels something resonating in them when the topic of irresponsibility comes up, the following is the best recommendation I can make for getting out of a bad place.

Take stock of where you actually sit, get professional help if you need it, and find out what the reality is. How good or bad is it? Refuse to act in the nebulous state of "we're still here aren't we" and know exactly what you have in assets and liabilities. Know exactly what you need to exist and how much you have beyond that or how much you fall short. You can then celebrate that things are good and enjoy being able to communicate much more clearly where you stand and what your needs are. Or you can confess to your community where you stand, take responsibility (ever noticed how stupid people sound when they confess to something and then blame someone or something else for their bad choices?), ask forgiveness, *and tell them what you are doing to get back on track.*

The reason that confession is so important is that the bad press that comes with exposure is worse. Confession takes guts and the courage to say "we screwed up" is tremendous. As a result, people respect when a confession is made. They may be temporarily horrified, but even in that moment they respect the confession and between the two emotional responses of horror and respect, it's the sense of respect that will last longer. The end result can be the ultimate comeback, standing stronger than ever.

When individuals or organizations are exposed and confess after the fact, they missed their opportunity. It will still go better for them if they face the music rather than making excuses, but there will be less respect to sustain them after the horror wears off. The chances of being able to make a comeback have been severely limited.

An individual or organization that is exposed *and* hides from the consequences… Well, it was nice knowing you, you're toast.

I do want to note that there is always hope for the bigger picture of one's life or the life of an organization. No one is ever completely helpless or hopeless. But there is no getting away from how far a fall it will be for those who are exposed and don't take responsibility for their actions at the time. For those who choose to take responsibility after some time has passed, there is an incredible amount of rebuilding that needs to happen to get back on a successful path, but it can be done. Taking responsibility is in fact the first step to really getting back on track!

Based on what I've seen behind the scenes I believe a lot of organizations avoid getting into details and avoid opportunities for donors to ask too many questions because they know they won't like the answers. And that practice needs to stop.

You don't have to fake happy answers when things go wrong to keep a donor community motivated. As mentioned earlier, it's the fake answers that are turning them off. They know there are problems. Be honest with them and do something about the problem and then your donor community is more likely to have your back while you work to make yourself better than ever. They'll trust you to get back on your feet.

8

IT'S RAINING
RESOURCES

Your organization will always need more than just money.

There is one concern I want to make sure is fully put to rest before we get into the more specific details of resource campaign techniques, and that is the fear of resources becoming a burden.

One of the reasons fundraising and gathering just money can be so enticing is that money doesn't take up a lot of space. It's in a lock-box, safe, or bank account and it makes keeping life neater and tidier easier. The concept of resource campaigning causes some people to picture having their offices flooded with *things*. Things that create extra work, that take up space, that aren't what was actually needed. And volunteers who don't know what they're doing making a muddle of things that were running so smoothly until they showed up. The heart of the concern is that *asking for and accepting resources in their various forms might make it harder to do our job.*

I will hopefully remove that concern by providing this example of an organization that clung to fundraising and chose to outright reject resource campaigning.

I read an online article from a food cupboard that was trying to communicate the importance of *just giving money to food initiatives.* The reasoning was that when food items are donated they are heavy, require storage, and often aren't the items the families actually need. It's not helpful to have shelves full of spaghetti when what a family really needs are diapers.

In addition, they highlighted that the food cupboards have corporate connections and staff who are professional couponers who can make a dollar stretch five times further. In other words, if you give us a can of beans we have a can of beans, but if you give us the money you would have paid we can turn that into five cans of beans.

There is absolutely some truth to these struggles and some insight for donors who enjoy supporting food cupboards. However, the organization who posted the article unintentionally pushed away a huge chunk of donors because the article failed to acknowledge that food cupboards also have a responsibility in clearly communicating their needs if they want to receive certain items and not others, and also didn't acknowledge other resource needs they have.

For now, think about this. Cash will help with things like purchasing needed food and paying the bills associated with the space they operate out of. That article they published caused them to miss out on all of the following opportunities.

Volunteers could potentially save money for the food cupboard through janitorial services or helping with their website updates. They may not want people to buy them food, but do they need lightbulbs for their office? Printer paper? A new floor mat inside the front door so people don't slip on their way in? If they are specific they can get exactly the items they need and put the money not spent on those items towards purchasing the food items they need to meet families' specific needs. Do they offer workshops on how to cook cheap and healthy meals or how to grow your own food which members of the public can pay to participate in? Those workshop fees would help to buy more food. Are they looking to connect with local gardeners so they can get more fresh produce? Are they looking to connect with a plumber because their sink is giving them trouble? Are they giving back to the community in some way and want people to know about it which would, in turn, gain them more gratitude and support from their neighbours?

Your organization will always need more than just money. It's okay if a ton of resources come in! Resource campaigns *think bigger and understand that while, yes, more work is involved, that work is absolutely worth the incredible return on investment! And it doesn't mean that you'll be buried in useless things or derailed by disruptive people.*

This next section exploring The 6 Key Resource Categories is going to be primarily focused on the foundational principles that will help you be successful in pursuing each form of resources. There will be less focus on more specific how-to's which will be found later in the chapter on Transitional Change and the appendices!

This is very much grocery store time, an opportunity to wander the aisles and view the ideas on the shelves. If you see something enticing, grab hold of it! If it looks awful, leave it on the shelf and keep walking. It's okay to love, like, disagree with, and even hate some of the concepts coming up. I won't ask you to agree with everything I'm proposing, but I will ask you to at least consider it before walking by. Everything that has been included in this book has been shared here for a reason. I've seen the behind-the-scenes, long-term pictures for enough organizations to say that I wouldn't leave a single one of these concepts out of any campaigns under my care.

I would also suggest not letting the amount of information overwhelm you if you're starting to feel like implementing resource campaigns for yourself or your organization would be too much. No one said you have to apply everything all in one go. You can transition, making course adjustments to what you're doing now so you can slowly see more and more positive responses. If you want to dive in you can do that, but you can also take small steps over time and get to the same great place.

9

PURCHASED SERVICES/PRODUCTS

These relationships thrive when your organization says 'this is what we have to offer' and people can pay for it. These donors enjoy the reciprocal relationship of having given something and received something of value.

These donors get *angry* if simply asked for money with nothing offered in return. They want to know how you are earning your way and care deeply about fiscal responsibility.

PURCHASED SERVICES/PRODUCTS (+17%)

These relationships thrive when your organization says 'this is what we have to offer' and people can pay for it. These donors enjoy the reciprocal relationship of having given something and received something of value.

These donors get *angry* if simply asked for money with nothing offered in return. They want to know how you are earning your way and care deeply about fiscal responsibility.

To start off, chocolate-bar fundraisers and other strategies that involve selling something to family, friends and neighbours, have actually been using a resource campaign tool! Anyone offering a chocolate bar in exchange for money is not asking for no-strings-attached funds because you gave the donor chocolate! It's a Purchased Services/Products donation!

However, if a resource campaign tool is used while operating with a fundraising mentality it will once again create a yes/no equation with a 17/83 split! If someone selling chocolate bars does not mention all the other ways to give then the only question being posed to someone who answered their doorbell is, "Do you want to buy a chocolate bar" and for 83% of the people you ask the answer will be, "No". Because they weren't asked for specific items, time, money, connections or gratitude the only thing they know when asked the question is that they don't want the chocolate! The better we grab ahold of the concepts behind resource campaigning the better we can use the same tools we've already been using to achieve better results!!! With resource campaigns, we go out with a comprehensive strategy that means not everyone will buy a chocolate bar, but every person we connect with will give us *something* to support our cause.

Let's explore some foundational principles that will help you make the most of connecting with this donor category.

1. WHATEVER YOU HAVE TO OFFER THAT PEOPLE WILL PAY FOR, YOU HAVE MORE

Organizations who don't offer services or products that people can pay for because they don't think they have anything to offer either need to change their perspective or request some outside help. Because not only do they have something, they've always got more when they stop and think about it. Don't believe me? Create a list of everything you could offer that people would be willing to pay for. Come on, give it a try! Now ask the question, "What else could we do?" In fact, ask that question five more times. You just added five more things to your list didn't you? There is always more. Here are just a few ideas:

- Rental fees earned through space, equipment, or resources for rent

- Registration fees earned through workshops, retreats, or camp programs offered

- Ticket sales or pass-the-hat for performances, speakers, presentations, or special events

- Professional fees for services rendered

  - Ex. If your organization provides legal support for homeless youth could you charge to provide legal services for families whose teen gets into trouble?

- Fees collected for providing a unique experience such as restricted access, behind-the-scenes tours, a-day-in-the-life-of, etc?

If you are not familiar with a-day-in-the-life-of experiences, these are opportunities created to live life from someone else's perspective for a window of time. If your organization is the steward of a historical site what a perfect opportunity to charge people to be guided through a day that reflects what their lives would have been like living there. If your organization supports the homeless it's a great opportunity to charge people to be guided through a day that reflects what their lives would be like if they were homeless.

I once spoke with a teenager whose church youth group participated in a 'homeless for a night' experience who shared what a deep impact it had on him. He was prepared to bring only what he could carry in a backpack and sleep behind a local grocery store, but unbeknownst to the group, the organization offering the event had made arrangements with the local police to have an officer come by in the early hours to tell them they couldn't stay there and to move on! This lead to a scramble and some group problem solving trying to figure out where they would go next and what to do. A guide was present to provide help and ensure safety if needed, but otherwise was simply there and did not interfere. The youth debriefed in the morning and went home with a new take on what it was like to live on the streets and how grateful they were for the safe homes and comfortable beds they had. Any number of parents are willing to pay for their child to have that kind of experience.

2. OFFER PRODUCTS OR SERVICES THAT MATCH YOUR VALUES

It would be a little weird if someone asked you to buy a chocolate bar to support their healthy living initiative. What? So let's take a look at the different outcomes you can experience if you provide products and services that are in conflict with, simply disconnected from, or totally in tune with your organization's values!

CONFLICTING VALUES:
Having a bachelor auction to support ending human trafficking sends a very confusing message. What is being offered is in conflict with the supposed values. People can question if the organization is actually clear about its values and mission. When we don't feel confident that someone knows where they are going and why they are going there we are less likely to want to connect with them. There is an element of distrust or just plain confusion about who you are and what there is to connect with in the first place. Offering products or services in conflict with your values tends to result in failure to connect with as many donors as you could have otherwise and to cause damage to connections with existing donors. This is not the way you want to go.

DISCONNECTED VALUES:
If that same organization offered products and services such as a poinsettia campaign around Christmas or an annual basketball tournament there is absolutely opportunity for resources to come in. However, poinsettias and basketball have nothing to do with their values surrounding ending human trafficking. Flowers and basketball aren't in conflict with their values, but a bigger opportunity is missed when the *environment and the experience* don't match the message being shared. Remember the art of facilitation? If you *talk* about ending human trafficking and then *play* basketball, guess which experience speaks louder to the donors? The players and crowd take more away from the experience of the game than they will from hearing about your cause. Buying flowers has barely any experience to it at all. Whoever a person buys flowers from, now they have flowers. Your cause can become a background element, the place where the resources *just happen to be going* after the event or sale and so whether people buy flowers or play basketball to support your cause or someone else's matters little. This is also not the way you want to go.

CONNECTED VALUES:
So let's use facilitation to your advantage. You know what your values are. You know what your mission is. When choosing what products or services to offer to donors always be sure to create an *environment and an experience that match your values and mission.* That same organization offering tickets for an evening event with guest speakers who have experience with human trafficking would not only help to bring in resources but would also be offering a service, an event, that matches the values and mission of the organization! This ultimately meets current needs and helps to build people's long-term connection with the organization and its mission. Learning directly from someone who has escaped the sex trade, a nurse who has rescued sex workers when they came to the hospital for healthcare, and someone who has completed a jail sentence for human trafficking and has reformed their ways is going to make for an evening that people will not soon forget! They're more likely to see the value of what you do and are more likely to support you for the long-term.

What do you stand for? Why do you exist? What are you trying to achieve? And what can you offer people that is in line with that?

Can you imagine if sports teams stopped selling high-sugar food products and instead started selling sports equipment? Buy a soccer ball to support your local soccer team! Buy a hockey stick to support your local hockey team! Everyone has something that can be offered that is in line with what they are most passionate about!

3. OFFER PRODUCTS OR SERVICES THAT HAVE VALUE TO THE DONOR

Nobody likes to be given crap. People are even less inclined to *pay* for crap. When those boxes of chocolates start being sent out into the neighbourhood to support a local school club or team, are those students going around with chocolate or chocolate-flavoured wax compound?

When you offer to rent space at your facility for meetings is it clean, with clear instructions for how to use the features in the room and a friendly face to welcome them to the space? Or is it kind of gross from when your team used it earlier and the group just comes and goes without being acknowledged by anyone?

If you are going to offer something ask what would truly make it valuable to the people you are offering it to. It doesn't mean the item has to be perfect. Someone might very happily pay $100 for a quilt made by a local children's troop. The stitching is uneven, the pattern is somewhat askew, and the cotton batting is peaking out on one corner, but what makes it valuable is that the kids' best efforts were put into it and that is heartwarming and valuable to the person who buys it. I once paid to support a Kickstarter campaign called *50 Kids. 50 Cameras*. With my support 50 kids living in a slum in Brazil would participate in a five-week photography workshop, empowering them to share their stories of growing up there, and I would receive a copy of one of the pictures taken from their perspective. The picture I received is of a group of people standing in front of hanging blankets and laundry. The one woman who is the focus of the picture is looking down towards the little photographer but is distracted by something else as a child reaches for the object she is holding in her hands. It's a candid photo of a moment in life. It's slightly blurry and perfect. I love it.

Sometimes the value of something comes from its quality, and other times it comes from the heart put into it or the fact that it's unique. What makes what you have to offer valuable?

If you are looking for inspiration, great ideas for things you can offer your donor community in exchange for their support, Kickstarter is an amazing place to explore. Look not only at the projects people are trying to complete, but the rewards they are offering for the various levels of support. Kickstarter is the ultimate hive for Purchased Services/Products donors!!! They love being able to say they gave money and got something awesome in return. They aren't buying the item the same way they would buy it from the store. They are buying something knowing that ultimately they are making it possible for the person, team or organization running the campaign to achieve a goal of their own. To create a game. To perform on a national stage. To reach a community in the depth of the jungle. And more. People who want to buy something new and interesting to benefit themselves shop from stores. People who want to buy something new and interesting to benefit themselves *and others* shop through Kickstarter.

Get inspired at www.kickstarter.com.

4. STOP MAKING CRAP

Steve Jobs infamously told Nike that they made a lot of good things, but they also made a lot of crap. Stop making crap. That advice paid off.

Putting things out there just for the sake of having options is not good practice and you will create a drain on your resources as well as gain a bad reputation in some corners. You can have more affordable items available for people to have options, but still, make sure the affordable items have quality.

Camp tuck shops are notorious for this sort of thing. The richer kids can buy the $90 hoodie and the poorer kids can buy a pen for $2. If it's a good pen then it's a perfect option. If it's a crappy pen, you just insulted the poor kid and communicated to the rich kid that you make crap (they just didn't find themselves in the position of that being the only option available to them).

Have *great stuff only*. To keep crap off your shelves always ask manufacturers for samples before placing orders and don't place an official order until you've held the sample in your hands and asked yourself 'does this feel good' or 'does this make me happy'? People are tactile and it doesn't matter how good something looks, if it doesn't feel good then our relationship with that item sours and so does our relationship with who we got it from on some level. Is it quality? Does it feel good? Will it last? If the answers are yes, yes, and yes then chances are you've found what you're looking for. If the answer to any of those questions is no, then keep looking.

It's also beneficial to remember that when any company tries to sell you an item saying it is great for promoting your business… promoting your business is *their business*. They might know something is crap, but they also know people are willing to pay for it to get their name out there. Always be wary anytime somebody says something would be a good purchase for you if they are the ones who would financially benefit if you do!

If you offer a service of some kind instead of a product make sure the service is quality. Put your best people forward. Train people and invest in their development so they keep getting better at what they do. Plan ahead so that the experience is smooth. Look at the questions people ask and use those questions to fill in the blanks of your communications (ex. If people keep asking what time your tour starts it means it's not easy to find information. Make it easier to find!). Experiences can be crappy too. Ask yourself, if you participated in the service you're offering, would you feel like you got your money's worth or feel like you wasted your time and money?

The Cost of Crap

The nice thing about crap is that it's cheap. That's the main driving concept behind sales of garbage with organization's logos printed on it for promotion or trinkets distributed as gifts. But crap isn't cheap. Far from it. In fact, crap comes with a higher cost than many people realize. Here's a sample scenario to try and drive the point home.

If a restaurant served family meals and had the children's meals bundled up in a fun box with a toy, that could be pretty great motivation for a family to want to eat at that restaurant on a semi-regular basis. Let's say this restaurant is big enough and has enough locations that it sells one million of its children's meals every year and has been in operation for fifty years.

That's fifty million children's toys that are now in circulation today. These fifty million toys are all variations of plastic and metal and with various abilities to stand independently, roll, move their arms, or jump if you press a button. Pretty simple stuff. But colourful and usually a reflection of some current trend like a movie out right now so it seems to be making kids (and therefore their parents) happy. But fifty million chunks of colourful plastic in circulation leads to some additional questions.

How many kids continue to play with all of the toys they have in their possession? Are those toys still useful to their owners today?

How many of those toys are still functional today and survived being used and the passage of time? How many of the 50-year-old toys are still able to be played with?

How much plastic and metal did it take to make those 50 million toys? How much is the cost of the creation of the toys contributing to the prices that restaurant charges for their food?

How much storage space does the restaurant chain require to manage that many toys? Does it cost them money to store those toys? Do they have to pay for space to store other items that could be stored where the toys are kept if the toys were not a part of the picture?

How much strain was put on the environment in order to make all of these toys? How much oil was harvested, how much pollution pumped into the air while processing, how much water polluted, how much gas burned during transportation?

How much strain will be put on the environment when the toys are disposed of? How long will it take for the materials to return to the earth? Who is going to be impacted by rotting, broken, partially decomposed toys being in their area? Will this impact adults? Children? Fish? Birds? Will it impact anyone's water quality or ability to safely or comfortably use a space in their community? How much space is the waste going to take up?

Now, what if this restaurant had a huge heart for children and for that reason created a children's charity? They particularly want to see children thrive in school and create support resources for students who are struggling. Their impact ends up being incredible with families and schools around the globe thankful for their hearts and hard work.

Now, what if the restaurant had a lightbulb moment and realized that the toys they are giving away in their meals are crap? They didn't intend to hand out crap, but now that they look at the bigger picture of how much it's costing them and where they actually want to see their money go (into profits and benefiting children struggling in school), they realize that crap has got to go.

Stopping to think about what they could give that matches with their values and that provides value to their young customers they might have another lightbulb moment. What does nearly every young kid do on their birthday when handed a stack of presents that drives their parents crazy? *They ignore the toy and play with the box.* Wait a minute…

If the restaurant starts investing their efforts into making the *box* the gift then all of a sudden a few crazy things start to happen. They start coming up with creative designs that can be punched out of the box which is now being made with perforated lines. Kids can now punch out cardboard dolls, cars, planes, and more. They still get to play with figures, but they're cardboard. Maybe part of the box can be punched out, folded, and inserted into a slot on the side to transform the box into a castle, or a car garage, or a spaceship. Families are more interested than ever. They love the creativity! (They also love that when their kid is done with it they can put the whole thing in their recycling or compost because the restaurant chose environmentally responsible materials. No more having to truck abandoned toys to the local thrift store, garage sale them or throw them out. Huzzah!)

On the corporate side of things, the restaurant is noticing that they're saving a *lot* of money. The boxes are costing them a bit more to get the right artwork and box design, along with the new perforated lines that need to be included, but these costs are nothing compared to the money being saved from stopping production of the toys.

In fact, those toys had been costing even more than they realized. They are no longer paying for design, manufacturing, transportation, or storage. They have so much more space available to them! Their restaurants feel less cramped and are better organized now that the toys don't need their own space.

And with their heart for children they've now found themselves with an incredible increase in net income which can be channelled to help even more families in need.

How many pens has your organization distributed over the years? How many stress balls, mugs, fridge magnets, notepads, keychains, and more? It's time to stop. Better things are waiting for you if you do.

Filter Questions to Help You Stop Buying or Making Crap

- Is anyone trying to sell us promotional or gift items saying they will benefit our organization?
- Is the person/company trying to convince us to buy these things going to financially benefit if we make that purchase?
- Do they have our best interests in mind or are they trying to sell us their products?
- Do the companies we work with have high-quality options or do they just sell crap?
- Are there any additional companies we can work with who we know will provide us with a high-quality product?
- Is there any way we can transform our current promotional items or gifts into a more quality product that matches our values and provides value to the recipients?
- Will the things we give either return to the earth within our generation or is it of high enough quality to be treasured for multiple generations?
- Do we need to give people anything at all or is that a practice everyone would benefit from if we stopped?

5. NEVER TAKE ON MORE THAN YOU CAN SUSTAIN WITHOUT THE HELP OF DONORS

Are you buying new property? Okay, how much will the new property taxes be and can your organization afford to take that on as part of their bare-bones requirements? Do your purchased services that pay for your existence bring in enough income to cover this additional amount? You say you're going to use the property to expand your services. How? Who is your target market? Are you planning on charging more for your services? Are you going to start offering something new? Are there other expenses associated with those changes?

When you have an initiative you're really excited about it's easy to view people who ask these kinds of questions as party-poopers, but they're really not. They'll go nuts celebrating, and maybe even buy the champagne if you can demonstrate that purchases with long-term financial consequences have been well thought out and planned for in advance. They aren't the people who refuse to have any fun or get excited, but instead are the voice of wisdom pointing out that your numbers don't add up, you're leaving too much to chance, and your excitement is taking you right towards some sharp pointy rocks that are going to hurt everyone involved.

There is an ancient proverb that says 'an enemy multiplies kisses, but wounds from a friend can be trusted'. An enemy will cheer you on all the way to you walking right off a cliff, but a friend will risk being the party-pooper to save you from your demise.

And taking on more than can be sustained without the help of donors has been the demise of many an organization. In fact, I think we're coming up on an era where more and more organizations who can not prove they are earning their way, maintaining their existence without requiring gifts to do so, will be vilified and gifts will stop coming in. I think many big organizations who don't change their ways now are going to find that their cultural climate around gift-giving will change rapidly and soon. If they aren't already steering a course in the right direction they may find they can't adjust their practices fast enough to keep their doors open. Be ready now!

Camp IAWAH

Camping, Outdoor Education & Retreating

Camp IAWAH is a Christian camping ministry with a beautiful property for people to enjoy nature, excellent facilities and program options that bring people together in community, and a big heart for the people they serve.

Many low-income campers experience the benefits of attending IAWAH's programs at heavily subsidized rates and part of what makes this possible is that the quality of programming is so high it leads many others to happily pay for their experience in full.

IAWAH charges money to provide camp programs, outdoor education experiences for schools, and retreats for groups year-round. They use their resources to create sources of income that are in tune with their values, allowing them to achieve their mission and earn revenue at the same time.

Quality matters to the organization and for that reason people who participate in their programs are likely to return. Their resulting donor community is now made up of generations of donors who were so happy with their experience that they pay for their children and grandchildren to go as the years go by. When people give money to this organization the consistent message is that they are more than satisfied with what they received in return.

Learn More:

www.iawah.com

2045
MY FUTURE PREDICTION FOR COLLEGES & UNIVERSITIES

The conversations around post-secondary education have changed dramatically in a short period of time. A generation ago the most pertinent question helping people choose the institution they wanted to attend was, "where will I get the best *education*". For this generation, the question changed to "where will I get the best *experience*?" Endure uncomfortable dorm conditions to get a great education? Not anymore! Dorm comfort is now a make-or-break consideration when choosing a post-secondary institution. If someone is willing to travel then multiple institutions usually offer the program an applicant is looking for. It's the proposed experience they'll receive that decides who the top contender is.

Within the next generation, I see strong evidence that we're going to see another turnover in motivation as youth start asking,"where will I receive *the greatest value for my time and money*", and I don't think the majority of colleges and universities are ready for it.

The next generation rising up cares deeply about fiscal responsibility, about sustainability, about minimal living, and taking on life to the full without the burden of crushing debt. Why? Because they are being raised by people whose length of life and quality of life are being decreased by the consequences associated with debt, *first incurred in the form of student loans*.

Youth who once looked to the government to solve the problem of burdensome debt through subsidies, improved student loan programs, and even free post-secondary education are now *questioning what the point of post-secondary education is at all*. Why not just enter the field you're interested in and learn hands-on? Or even better, why not create your own job? Why not have a life where living and making a living are the same the thing?

This upcoming generation is surrounded by influential voices telling them about the value of real-life experience. Tim Ferris, the author of *Tools of Titans*, speaks very convincingly about getting a 'real world MBA' rather than learning within a formal institution. This message resonates deeply with a lot of people and is shaping the mindset of youth who not only hear more and more influencers talking about learning through living, but also hear their parents lament that they didn't know or think to take that path themselves.

This generation has more tools at their disposal to create their own sources of income than ever before, no longer having to rely on local economy, but having opportunity to create a sustainable income through the global reach of the internet. Even those who intend to work for others have greater clarity that they could ask for a job today and be told to show up for orientation on Monday, or go to school for four years, be $75,000 in debt, and still be told to show up for orientation on Monday. What would they have to show for those years dedicated and the money spent?

Are the time I dedicate and the money I spend going to be worth what I get out of the learning opportunity both during and after?

If colleges and universities don't change their ways quickly the resounding answer will be *no*.

$5000 per semester? $10,000 per school year? Oh wait, that doesn't even include required student fees, books, or room and board. And I'll actually be making how much afterwards? At what expense to my health, wellbeing, and quality of life in the long-term? What other expenses will I have in the meantime? What if I already have other financial commitments or people to care for? Does this form of education fit into my life and enhance the quality of it? Or does it ask me to work my life around it and decrease my ability to enjoy everything else that makes my life worth living like time with family and friends, travel, hobbies, sports, and rest?

Time and money are precious commodities up-and-coming youth are going to refuse to part with easily. As they see it, current post-secondary fees and learning structures ask students to miss out on life in the form of time spent sitting at a desk or in a lecture hall rather than *doing*. It asks students to miss out on life in the form of working Mcjobs that are not in line with their vision for their life, but don't require a degree and let them earn tuition money. This means that while employed where they are unsatisfied they also miss out on time with people and time doing things that do make them feel satisfied with life. Student loans ask those who make use of them to miss out on time with their spouse and children because of trying to work to pay off the debt and get back on track for other large purchases such as buying their first home. It asks them to work even harder because while paying off student loans and mortgages they still somehow need to prepare for retirement. This is what their parents are doing. *And they don't want that.*

Obviously, there is a much larger picture of financial decisions and financial skills at work here for which post-secondary institutions are not fully to blame. People don't have to live a life of work, debt and drudgery to attend and pay for a few years of post-secondary education. But it's happened to enough people that the next generation is paying attention and looking for institutions that can honestly say they are financially responsible, not asking for more than they need to, and providing services that are a quality return on investment. What does this mean for when the year 2045 rolls around?

I think students are going to start openly rejecting the tuition schools are charging and the time structure of semesters. Instead of looking for solutions to find the money needed, their energies are going to be devoted to looking for other ways to learn and gain experience. Anyone still interested in attending a formal institution is going to be looking for who is charging the least in combination with providing the best education that reflects living life rather than putting life on hold.

Post-secondary institutions that have become gluttonous financial vacuums because of expansions sustained by past donations are going to be starved down to a smaller size or close their doors as those donations dry up. The older generations who believed in loyalty and giving to one's alma mater for life will pass away and the younger generations will be looking at institutions asking them how they are *earning* their way. Upcoming youth will have about as much interest in giving money to a post-secondary institution as they would to giving money to a local gym. Despite their non-profit status, post-secondary institutions will be viewed as corporate entities who need to earn their way or go under and those institutions who continue to ask for gifts will be vilified.

People are going to be looking for reasonable fees that fit within a sustainable budget and reasonable time structures that fit within a sustainable lifestyle. I predict that the post-secondary institutions who survive the coming changes will do so because they will have moved to one of two delivery models:

1. Subscription-based
2. Earn-and-learn

For youth looking to pay for education they're going to be looking for where they can pay no more than $250 per month to attend and where they can attend class when it works for them. You read that right. Students are going to be looking for places that would cost them no more than $3000 for an entire calendar year and that work around their lives!

This subscription model makes education affordable *now* with a pay-as-you-go approach which addresses the next generation's money concerns, and breaks away from the outdated concept of education being measured in semesters, requiring people to learn during certain windows and structure the rest of their lives around an institution's schedule.

For youth looking for opportunities where they can make a living while learning the necessary skills they are going to be looking for institutions that have partnered with companies so that they receive training while being paid. They want to be paid for the time they put in, not to pay someone else.

This earn-and-learn model would eradicate the concept of being a post-secondary 'student', and transform those accepted to the institution into employees! People would not apply for programs, but for careers, researching what companies or regulating bodies are partnered with which post-secondary institutions so they can apply for jobs where they will earn-and-learn.

This model also creates all sorts of opportunities for universities to sustain their facilities rather than having to give them up as financial gifts dry up. A bio-lab which was a school classroom with a professor could become a satellite location for a bio-company that would use the lab to train new employees who can go on to work at their other locations. It becomes a functional wing of a broader company that happens to operate out of a 'campus'. Campuses have the opportunity to become thriving mega-malls of goods and services where incredible collections of companies are gathered in close-quarters because they are using the facilities to train their new recruits. The most complex and rigid programs will likely be the slowest to adapt, but in the end even programs for medical practitioners and engineers can (and will have to) adapt to the idea that people want to earn-and-learn. They don't want to put their lives on hold for years at a time so they can then start making a living and paying off their obscene amounts of debt. A generation is rising up that would rather learn what they need to learn over 25 years of hands-on experience, living and learning, and being paid during that time than cram everything they've been told they need to get started into 4-10+ years of stress and waiting for their lives to start.

I think that when the year 2045 rolls around we are going to be shocked by how the post-secondary landscape has changed based on which organizations were able to answer the questions about what their bare bones structure is and how they are *earning their ability to exist.*

Will they have created a business model that demonstrates they *value students' time and money and therefore create the best value for investment that they can,* earning their ability to keep their doors open?

Will they have moved to a model that reflects people's desire to have earning and learning as *an integrated part of their lives, rather than putting their lives on hold so that they can learn and then earn*?

If you are a college or university, is your institution ready for this coming change?

10

SPECIFIC ITEMS

These relationships thrive when your organization shares a specific need and people can step up by purchasing the item, giving or lending from their own personal resources, or giving you the money to make the purchase.

These relationships are *deeply injured* when a gift is not used in the manner they understood it would be, if a gift that is important to them is turned down, if an item lent to you is not cared for properly, or if asked for money without being given a clear account of how that money will be used.

SPECIFC ITEMS (+17%)

> These relationships thrive when your organization shares a specific need and people can step up by purchasing the item, giving or lending from their own personal resources, or giving you the money to make the purchase.
>
> These relationships are *deeply injured* when a gift is not used in the manner they understood it would be, if a gift that is important to them is turned down, if an item lent to you is not cared for properly, or if asked for money without being given a clear account of how that money will be used.

Ever seen someone buy a meal for a homeless person instead of giving them the cash to buy it themselves? Or give money to a homeless person because they specifically said they need the money to buy new boots? These are your specific items donors!

Clear communication is critical for this category. Becoming intentional about incorporating specific items into your resource campaigning is going to be an ongoing masters level course in communication! And if you are willing to take on the challenge, navigate the speed bumps along the way, learn from both the good and bad experiences and keep growing then your jaw is going to be left on the floor by what resources you end up receiving!

Many organizations are already asking for specific items which is great! That's a fantastic start. The three reasons I see organizations failing to receive as many resources as they could are the following:

1. They haven't incorporated asking for specific items into a comprehensive resource campaign that takes into consideration all of The 6 Key Resource Categories.

2. They haven't worked closely with other members of their team who are responsible for overseeing other resource categories so they missed out on asking for additional things that would have been beneficial.

3. They ask for reasonable 'medium' things, but are concerned about asking for something too big or too small and therefore make the choice to not ask for those things at all.

The following principles will help you to make the most of this category and over time find yourself pleasantly overwhelmed with the generosity of your donor community.

1. SUCCESS REQUIRES BEING *EXACT* ABOUT THE DETAILS

If you ask your donor community to help you accomplish your mission by assisting with printer cartridges because you go through a lot of ink, that's a great idea! And it's fairly well known that printers require very specific cartridges so obviously, you need to tell your donors the brand and/or code and the needed colour(s) to make sure you receive the right ones.

Now, what if you ask your donor community for chairs? At first, it seems natural that to ask for chairs would be a pretty straightforward request. Until the chairs start arriving. You are now the proud owner of 10 metal folding chairs, 4 plastic deck chairs, 1 stuffed armchair, 2 reclining chairs, 14 wooden dining room chairs, and 8 padded dining room chairs. What kind of chair did you need? Did you get enough? And what are you going to do with all the other ones you now have kicking around…?

Provide donors with the exact number you need (if you know it), the condition it needs to be in (new, excellent, good, junk), the materials, size, colour, texture, age, brand, anything that you can think of that narrows the field to the kind of item you are actually looking for. The more information you can provide the more likely you are to get things that are useful, reduce headaches for your team, and reduce chances for donors to be hurt when you have to reject a gift or they find out you took it to the dump instead of using it for your mission.

2. PEOPLE HAVE DIFFERENT INTERPRETATIONS OF WHAT "EXCELLENT" MEANS. DON'T JUDGE.

No matter how clear you are about the condition you need something to be in, people's interpretations of the terms 'excellent', 'good', etc are all different. If you asked for donations of books in excellent condition and someone brings you a box of books that are all beaten up and water-stained, please still say thank you! Rather than assuming they didn't read your request carefully (or at all) or that they don't care, you'll better preserve your relationship with them if you assume that to them these books are still 'excellent'. You'll have to figure out what to do from there one circumstance at a time. Do you accept the donation or share that you're not able to take them at this time if it would genuinely be a burden to you? Every time this happens just make sure that you *learn from it*. Boost your communication skills. Don't blame the giver. Go back to your website and posters and see if you clarified what 'excellent' means. Did you say it meant no bent spines, no writing on the inside, no water stains, and no folded corners, or did you just say 'excellent'? I told you this was going to be a masters level course in communication skills! Going back to the first point about being exact, the more clear you can be about expectations of quality the fewer uncomfortable incidents you'll have of people showing up with something that doesn't meet the standard.

What makes for even more fun conversations is when donors suggest their gift is 'good enough'. "If you need a tractor this one will do the job," they say as they point in the direction of something that looks more like a tractor-shaped rust sculpture. Don't worry. It's okay to say you're looking for great rather than good enough! Some people will be offended by the idea that you'd ask for something nicer rather than taking what you're offered, but that has to do with their family or cultural history, that's not on you. If you'd prefer to not give your staff tetanus, but you also don't want to lose the relationship with the person offering you the rust tractor, you can always respond with something like this:

"Thank you for the offer! Our team has a more specific need that this particular tractor does not meet so we won't be taking it at this time. However, your spirit of generosity is a big blessing to our organization and for that, we are truly grateful."

3. TAKE INTO CONSIDERATION THE BIG PICTURE

If you ask for a piano, trust me, you'll get a piano. There are any number of people who would be happy to pass on the instrument gathering dust in their living room that they just don't play anymore. But that piano is either going to be a blessing or a liability depending on how you worded the request.

Assuming you've been exact about your request and someone has contacted you offering just what you need then there's still quite a few things to figure out.

Are they responsible for moving it? Are you responsible for moving it? Do you need to hire a piano moving company? Do you need to ask for volunteer piano movers? If it goes out of tune from being moved who is going to tune the piano after the move? Someone within your organization? Do you need to hire a piano tuner? Ask for a volunteer piano tuner? What pathway does the piano need to follow through your building to get to its new home? Does anything need to be cleared out of the way? Are the doorways wide enough or is a renovation involved to get it in?

Any time you ask for an item look at the big picture before you publish the request. Know what additional needs there are inherent to receiving the item and maintaining it so you don't find that a free item costs you more than expected. If you have additional needs, include them as part of the original request rather than as an afterthought!

Speaking of which, please also always consider long-term maintenance when taking on any item, whether you buy it or it is donated. Does the item need to be inspected, professionally cleaned, or insured? Will it increase how much you pay in taxes, bills, or rent? What are the costs associated with disposing of it once it has outlived its usefulness? That free chest freezer that isn't Energy Star approved might add some bulk to your hydro bills. That boat might not be worth it if your insurance company thinks it's a higher risk item and increases your fees by a few hundred dollars a year.

Thinking about the big picture will not only help you to be intentional about what you ask for and help you communicate more clearly, but it may even change your perspective on what you think you want or need in the first place. Grab some coffee, sit down, and give this one some thought. You'll be glad you did.

4. HAVE A SYSTEM IN PLACE TO TELL PEOPLE WHEN YOU HAVE ENOUGH

Donors who give in the form of specific items can have their feelings, and therefore your relationship with them, deeply injured if they go to the trouble of getting you a gift only to have you say, "Oh, actually, we already have one." When it comes to having extra paper towels or a spare can opener for your kitchen it's not the end of the world to accept extras, and it can be worth it to preserve the relationship. But if someone gave up a portion of their vacation fund because they wanted to buy you the entire suite of waiting room furniture you asked for from a furniture store only to find out you don't need them, can't take them, and the store doesn't do returns… then you're going to have a very unhappy camper on your hands and severe damage to the relationship.

If you are going to include asking for specific items in your resource campaigning (and you are because otherwise you're not truly setting yourself up for success) then you have to have someone who is dedicated to monitoring the needs being met and updating communications as quickly as possible to avoid duplicate donations where that is not beneficial.

A good communication tool to use for larger requests is to ask people to contact you first if they are considering giving that specific item. It provides a buffer in between the person seeing the need and trying to fulfill it right away which might be the time your organization needs to avoid a disaster.

Mess up on this once and it will be a good lesson to never do it again. Learn from the experience if it happens and then move forward.

5. USE EXISTING REGISTRIES OR CREATE ONE!

We usually call them wedding registries or baby registries, but when you walk into a department store that has a hand-held unit so you can walk around the store scanning the codes on the packages of things you want so you can build your list, you can scan *anything*. Most large department stores have made it possible for people to buy the items in store or online and give you an online account so you can manage the items and requested numbers or even create the registry from the comfort of your home or office.

Online sales portals such as Amazon have wish lists which again allow you to add anything you want and all you have to do is share the link to the list. Anyone can then hop on Amazon, choose what they would like to purchase on your behalf and have it delivered directly to you. Amazon has a wild array of options and if you need it, chances are it's somewhere on Amazon!

You can always create your own registry on your website by listing specific items you need and providing the link to the supplier. This requires a little bit more hands-on monitoring by someone on your team so that as things arrive the item requests can be updated on your site, but particularly for items you go through a lot of it might not be a bad thing to have some extra printer cartridges or rolls of toilet paper lying around if you just leave the request up as a permanent ongoing need.

Need items from a specific manufacturer or your geography makes it wiser to work with a local distributor, but they don't have a registry option? Schedule a meeting with them and ask them to make one for you! No company in its right mind will turn down that kind of request because you are essentially asking them, "Could I please send a large number of people to buy items from your store that we need?" When this kind of relationship is established you are now able to leverage your donor community by telling them where they can buy items that you need, and the store you are sending them to is more likely to post your wish list in-store or in their retail communications in the hopes that people will help you out, which now gives you access to their customer community!

What is particularly wonderful about creating a registry is that it respects the business' need to earn an income and not just give away everything they have. If you ask the store to give to you from their inventory and they say no, many organizations would try asking for a donation and if they got a no to both requests they would walk away thinking they had been unsuccessful. That's old fundraising mentality at work. Yes, they were unsuccessful, but the only reason they were unsuccessful is that they asked for donations from only two of The 6 Key Resource Categories. Sharing all of your needs when you approach a local store gives them the opportunity to help in the way that resonates with them (you might end up with a store manager offering to volunteer for a role you needed filled!). If as part of that you ask a company to set up a registry, you are asking for their Gratitude! You're showing you appreciate their business and want to channel people their way, they respond with gratitude by setting up the registry for you which they otherwise wouldn't normally do and channel people to help you out because it helps them too. By tapping into the gratitude of the company a tool has now been created for other members of the community to purchase things and give specific items to you. The 6 Key Resource Categories reflect the synergy of the broader community and not just individuals!

What could this look like practically? Imagine a high school music teacher working with a bare-bones budget trying to keep a music program alive getting a phone call from the local music store that there is a saxophone for them to come pick up. Then a call that two scores of music they wanted have been ordered and should arrive by mail in the next two weeks. And now a flute is ready for pick up. The music teacher's resources slowly build over time and the music program grows stronger and stronger as a result! Seriously, what do you need? If you order food for your dining hall or cafeteria then talk to your food supplier about creating a registry. How amazing to find some extra non-perishable items added to your next order because someone bought them for you! If you need craft supplies imagine picking up items at the store that didn't cost you a penny because local crafters were excited to buy the exact items you said you needed while they were grabbing their own goodies. Creating registries benefits you, local businesses, and makes your donors who love to give through donating specific items exceptionally happy to be involved.

6. TELL PEOPLE HOW YOU *WILL USE* THE MONEY, NOT JUST HOW YOU *USED* IT

If you approach someone who likes to give specific items and ask them for money, thinking how great it will be when you send them your newsletter and show them how you used it, you've just lost 17% of your donor audience because these guys *hate* that. They view a person or organization who asks for money without being able to say up front what it's for as irresponsible or even worse, a trickster or liar. More is better? Heck no. "More is better" is NOT responsible financial planning and is a huge sign of fiscal irresponsibility. Anyone asking for money with no-strings-attached is not to be trusted and is probably going to spend it on something selfish or foolish.

Remember the earlier example of someone buying a meal for a homeless person instead of giving them cash? Many do it because they want to help, but without knowing exactly how the money will be used they often worry it will go towards alcohol or drugs. Buying the meal ensures the homeless person gets a meal. A Specific Items donor is more likely to give cash to a homeless person who says they want to buy some soup and a bun at the cafe they are standing in front of. Even more so if the homeless person can say exactly how much that soup and bun will cost.

Many people who give in the form of specific items do so by giving the exact amount of money needed to pay for the specific item in question. Camps asking for people to donate money to a camp fund that pays for children from low-income families to attend for a week will only get a response from 17% of their donor community, the 17% who like to give funds. Camps asking for people to consider paying for one week of camp for a child from a low-income family will activate another 17% of their donor community who prefer to give specific items for a total of 34% engagement! That's a lot more resources being channelled towards that specific fund helping more kids come to camp. And chances are the total donated by Specific Items donors is going to be higher than that of the donors giving Money because the Specific Items donors knew *exactly* how much was needed. Give to your camp fund? Sure, here's $200. Give $575 to pay for a kid from a low-income family to go to your camp for a week? Sure, here's $575.

Another cool outcome of telling people up front how their money will be spent is that it often becomes the catalyst for donors creating mini-campaigns of their own. Their current personal resources may not add up to the needed amount, but now that they have a specific goal in mind they go for it.

The person you approached may sell a few things on Kijiji knowing that their old treadmill and that blender they don't use anymore are going to make it possible for a kid to go to camp. Or they might work with friends to make and sell a quilt to get the money or approach a few friends who they know love to give money to this sort of thing.

It gets even better when you have a range of things you're asking for with bigger and smaller price tags. Someone might not be willing to give you $5, but they'll give you $5 to buy granola bars for an after-school program snack. Someone might not be willing to give you $20, but they'll give you $20 to buy 40 saplings to be planted at a site that was deforested by a mining company. Someone might not be willing to give you $200, but they'll give you $200 to provide a medical worker overseas with a bicycle to get from one village to another.

Being able to 'buy' something specific by giving money that has a designated purpose also opens up a lot of doors for gift giving! In a world where more people are waking up to the benefits of minimalism and are realizing the *burden* that many physical gifts create on loved ones, more people are looking for meaningful gifts they can give that won't gather dust in someone's house. When organizations ask for money and say up front how it will be used to purchase specific items to accomplish their mission then it makes it possible for a little girl to get the birthday gift of a goat given to a family who needed it. She loves goats. How perfect! It makes it possible for someone who is passionate about the environment to get the gift of a shoreline being rehabilitated after an oil spill. That gift hits the spot!

Non-profit organizations have *a lot* of opportunities here to expand their reach and the resources needed to do it simply by saying up front how money will be used in ways both big and small.

7. ASK FOR YOUR BIGGEST NEED, SMALLEST NEED, AND EVERYTHING IN BETWEEN

The majority of organizations that I interact with have this awful word shooting their resource campaign efforts in the foot. It's the word 'reasonable'. They ask themselves what would be reasonable to ask for and as a result shave off the bottom and top of their list of needs which could mean they've shaved off hundreds, thousands, tens of thousands, or maybe even *millions* of dollars that someone would have been willing to give them in the form of specific items.

To make sure you're not doing this you need to make a list of everything you need, and I mean *everything*. My recommendation is to start by asking what is the smallest thing you need. And if you're not sure, write down 'pens' because everyone needs pens. You should never be spending your money on pens because believe me any number of people will give them to you because they have too many. Don't believe me? Tell your canvassers to ask anyone who is not interested in giving to your organization at this time if they can have a pen. I promise you they will come back with fistfuls of them. Next, write down the biggest thing you need and if a little leprechaun pops up on your shoulder and says it's not 'reasonable' to ask for that, you tell him to zip it and flick him off.

What do you need? A new house custom-built to be wheelchair accessible to expand the number of group homes you have to serve clients with special needs? A farm so you can grow your own food? Plane tickets? Horses? 3-D Printers? An SLR Camera? A climbing wall? A new gym so you can build the climbing wall? Good gravy, what expensive things to ask for. Do it! And why? Because you don't always have to save up or go into debt to get these things. There are people who will give it to you if you ask or give it to you for much less than you would have imagined.

In the 1950's an Ontario family was approached by a group of men asking if they would be willing to sell their farm property for $5000 so they could turn it into a camp. Another interested buyer had submitted a proposal for paying $30,000. The property had a winter home and summer home located on it, one overlooking a beautiful lake and the other right on its shores. Acres and acres of forest were within its borders.

And the family sold it to the men offering $5000.

The family moved across the lake to another piece of property where they built a large mansion and could see the thriving camp that developed on their old property, a camp that is still going strong today. That's a pretty crazy story, but here's where it gets even crazier.

50 years later the family did it again. A restoration ministry was looking for a house where they could host retreats and provide counselling for people who needed deep rest and to experience some healing through being provided with a safe space where they were spoiled a bit. If you think about the difference it makes to how restful a vacation is if you stay at a 1-star resort or a 5-star resort it meant they were looking for a 5-star kind of place, with multiple bedrooms for multiple guests, a large dining space for large group meals, large sitting areas to be able to run workshops... they needed a mansion. And when they approached this same family, the house

was gifted to them for *waaaaaay* below market value! That ministry has gone on to be life-saving for any number of people who have benefited from the services and support offered there over the years.

I won't give away the name of this family or the names of these organizations just so the family doesn't have more requests for their resources than they know what to do with. But the story needs to be shared because it's such an amazing example of the synergy of community, the very reason why we ask for all of The 6 Key Resource Categories, and why we always make sure we ask for our needs big and small. This is the story of a community where needs surfaced, people were willing to ask for those needs to be met, and people were willing to give and give *big*.

Don't be afraid to ask for something stupidly small. Don't be afraid to ask for something stupidly big. Because within your community are people who don't think those requests are stupid at all and if you ask, they will give.

Partners International Canada

Hope in Action Campaign

Partners International Canada describes itself as a Christian International Development charity equipping the church, empowering women and children, and transforming communities in the least-reached and least resourced regions of the world.

Through holistic development and Christian witness, they work exclusively with indigenous Christian partners for greater growth and ministry impact.

Partners International Canada is part of a global alliance with offices in the United States, United Kingdom, Japan, Australia, and Singapore gathering resources to support the work happening in 56 countries with 122 indigenous Christian ministries.

The idea is that people in the communities being served know the needs best and have greater ability to meet the needs because they understand the landscape, politics, language, traditions, and more.

Locals can apply to receive support from Partners International and Partners, in turn, reaches out to increase the number of resources that can be dispersed. One of the ways they do this is through their Hope in Action campaign.

Any time of year you can hop on their website and scroll through the online catalogue to decide if you would like to set a child free from generational debt (and therefore lifelong slavery) for $150! You can buy a malaria net for $20 and stop children from dying of the disease. Want to give big? $5000 will pay for a sustainable medical clinic to be established.

Partners International takes ground level support and accountability seriously and sends members of its team to the remotest corners of the earth. They brave any number of challenges in order to ensure that individuals and organizations pouring themselves into helping their people are receiving the support they need and ensure that the resources they've received are being used for their designated purpose. Donors who give to Partners International can have confidence that if they paid for a family to receive two cows, that a family who needs them desperately is going to get two cows.

Learn more:

www.partnersinternational.ca

https://hopeinaction.ca/

Read:

The Ends of the Earth by Phil Dempster

[Note: This book contains records of trips to ministry sites in war-torn regions, areas of extreme poverty, and zones rocked by natural disasters. It brings to life the work being done and the hearts behind it.]

https://www.smashwords.com/books/view/625003

11

TIME

These relationships thrive when your organization says it needs help and people have the opportunity to fulfill a specific role that has meaning to them.

These relationships are *deeply injured* any time the donor is asked to give money to demonstrate true commitment or to 'show they have skin in the game'.

TIME (+17%)

Time is money. We hear this phrase all the time, but it hasn't fully sunk in if an organization continues to prioritize finding money over finding volunteers. These are equal resources.

Volunteer hours are money in disguise! When someone gives their time to complete a task that needed to be done it frees up paid staff to accomplish other things. You didn't have to pay someone to do that task? That's money still in your hands. Sometimes a volunteer can give of their time and resources (ex. An interior designer providing the paint and decorations used to complete your new waiting room). Other times people can donate their skill set but are not in the position of being able to donate the tools needed because it would drain their financial resources (ex. An interior designer happy to paint and decorate who needs you to purchase the paint and decorations). Treat any additional resources as a wonderful bonus rather than something to expect as part of the package. The focus for these donors is giving of their *time*.

Roles within your organization that either exist or could be created if a volunteer were available to do it may include the following:

ADVISORY ROLES

You may have advisory positions in place to cover legal requirements (Ex. Board of Directors) or committees that focus on specific tasks or areas of expertise (Ex. Building Committee). Panels can provide wonderful professional development opportunities for your team if volunteers are willing to come in for an evening and field some questions. Expert advisors can be brought in to present or sit down for coffee to provide insight into a specific topic or challenge.

STRUCTURAL ROLES

These individuals often work behind the scenes or you only interact with them briefly before moving on to the next thing. And without them, your organization would be *toast*. What administrative needs do you have? Would you benefit from having someone providing reception or greeting? What about food services or housekeeping? I used to think it was a horrible thing to even think about asking someone to volunteer to clean a toilet and then I interacted with a handful of individuals who shared how passionate they are about cleaning. Gross messes don't seem to impact them the same way, and it's a source of very real satisfaction for them to make a space spotless for the people who need to use it. If having someone come in once a week to spruce up your space would be beneficial and free up other people's time to do other things or reduce how much you're paying for professional cleaning then it's worth asking for!

DELIVERY ROLES

These are the front line people who are helping to make what your organization does happen. These roles are going to be very specific to the mission of your organization. If you're a soup kitchen do you need more people collecting trays and wiping tables? If you're a thrift shop do you need more people sorting and washing donated items before they go on the racks? If you're an employment centre do you need more volunteers helping clients write a resume?

If your organization is able to offer room and board as part of a volunteer position (ex. Camp counsellor) then all sorts of possibilities open up for volunteering!

People go through times of transition in their lives and sometimes find themselves free when they are needed most. I know many adults, even those with children, who have been able to donate weeks or months of their time because a place to live and food were provided for them and their family.

If your organization is currently made up of paid staff only, known and trusted elements who you are used to working with, it can leave you with the question of whether asking for volunteers is biting off more than you can chew. Won't things get messy if you start bringing in other people? Of course it will. Welcome to interacting with human beings! It takes effort for us to learn how to work together and that means having lots of great and interesting conversations along the way as well as awkward, uncomfortable, and difficult ones.

You're probably going to have to communicate to a volunteer at some point that things just aren't working and their services are no longer needed. It's not going to be the best experience you've ever had. But if you decide to avoid engaging volunteers because it *will be* challenging at times and *might be* a hassle or uncomfortable from time to time, what a shame it would be to miss out on meeting the other twenty amazing people who would have been unique and memorable to work with.

People are messy. It's our nature to be complex. And that's one of the main things that makes life interesting and worth living! Maybe your organization has been rolling along with carefully chosen, paid staff only and you're thinking about dabbling in inviting volunteers to join you, or maybe you have hoards of volunteers in your ranks. Either way, the following guiding principles will be helpful.

1. THE MORE DETAILS YOU PROVIDE UP FRONT, THE MORE VOLUNTEERS YOU GET

I'm a First Aid Instructor Trainer who helps to bring up the next generation of first aid instructors in Eastern Ontario and one of the most common pieces of feedback I give to instructor candidates is *when asking for volunteers always explain up front what you are asking them to do.* In a first aid class a volunteer may be needed to demonstrate the recovery position and be rolled over on the floor, or have a splint tied on their arm, or the beginnings of a shoulder sling draped across their chest, or have the instructor wrap their arms around them to demonstrate abdominal thrusts for choking. Someone might be fine having a splint on their arm, but feel wildly uncomfortable having the instructor wrap their arms around them. Someone might be fine to stand for a shoulder sling demonstration, but the clothing they are wearing isn't ideal for being rolled on the floor. Saying upfront exactly what you need the volunteer to do (ex. I need a volunteer to lie on the floor, face up towards the ceiling, so I can roll them on their side in the recovery position) will have one of two effects. It will either result in more people volunteering because they know the parameters of the job, or fewer people volunteering but the person who steps forward is the right one for the job.

We can gain one further piece of insight from looking at penguins. Penguins will often push each other on the edge of an ice flow until one penguin falls in and then the group waits to see if he gets eaten by a polar bear or seal. If the penguin is devoured, they go swimming later. If the first guy is fine, the rest will jump in. They can't see the hazards so they have to wait for someone else to go in to feel confident that it's okay. If your organization has said it's looking for volunteers without expanding on what that means or what the role includes, people interpret the lack of information as potential danger. Wading into the unknown means you could get hurt. But if you can clear the water, posting detailed volunteer position descriptions with the time requirement, skill set or certifications needed, language needs, tasks that will be completed, etc then potential candidates can see there are no polar bears and are more likely to jump in.

The basic points to cover for optimum volunteer attraction will always be:

- Who are you looking for
- What do you need this person to do
- Why is this person needed
- Where will they need to go to do this task
- When do they need to be there
- How do they get started

2. IT'S OKAY TO SAY YOU NEED *GREAT* AND NOT JUST *GOOD ENOUGH*

A lot of organizations are afraid to ask for volunteers to take on certain jobs because they are convinced the person will become a liability. Ask for a volunteer to help with accounting? If they don't know the tax laws then your organization could be in a lot of trouble when audited. Ask someone to do the wiring for the new renovation? Electricity can be dangerous and wrongly installed wires could mean the building burns down! It is worries like these that lead organizations to decide it's not worth the risk and to call in (and pay for) the professionals.

The problem isn't the nature of the task, it's that the organizations struggle with communicating the exact nature of their need. If you can afford to take on a volunteer who is a rookie because you're okay with lower quality work while the person learns the ropes then say so. If the quality of the work doesn't really matter because a pile of logs is a pile of logs then you can say you'll take on anyone to pile those logs. But if you need someone who has at least 10 years experience, specific certifications, proper licenses, and the right tools for a specific job then *say so*.

I was once made aware of a work project that was being completed by four gentlemen who had volunteered their time and skills to complete a renovation. Between their schedules, all four of them were required in order to be able to complete the project within a timely window. One of them was a detail-oriented expert, two were skilled and experienced workers who cared about quality work, and the last was someone who could get the job done and was happy to say anything not actively falling over was good enough. The project was completed, but with a lot of strain on all the volunteers and in a longer period of time than originally anticipated. The main reason was that the work that was good enough for one volunteer was a travesty to the detail-oriented volunteer, and entire shifts were sometimes spent undoing the work of one to replace it with the work of the other. Could the project have been completed faster if they all just did things to their own standard? Yes. But the person who ended up using the space when it was finished absolutely benefited from the final product created by the detail-oriented volunteer's adjustments.

Human beings are funny creatures and working together as a team often presents challenges that are worth navigating together for the results we achieve in the end. However, sometimes we have the opportunity to be intentional upfront about who we place on any given team and that can help to set that team up for greater success. If you know that 'good enough' is not going to cut it you might want to clarify your communications regarding what you are asking for and wait a bit longer to have the right volunteer step up to fill that spot. It could mean your project is completed faster and save a lot of stress for your volunteers.

Worried you'll offend someone? If someone offers you their help and you know the quality of their work is not going to cut it you can thank them for offering their services and let them know you are gathering a couple of options so the organization can see who is the best fit. You'll write down their name and get back to them if it seems like they are the best person to help meet the need. You can still build goodwill by thanking someone for an *offer* even if you don't take them up on it.

3. REMEMBER VOLUNTOLDS ARE NOT THE SAME AS VOLUNTEERS

Another piece of advice I give to first aid instructors is *never voluntell a person to do anything*. Always ask. It's for the same reasons as listed in the first point. Telling someone you need them to come up to the front for a demonstration or allowing another student to say "Bob will do it" is not good practice. That penguin just got pushed and is potentially convinced he's going to die. The stress associated with being voluntold is actually very high and when someone is focused on surviving it makes it very difficult for them to learn. A stressed out participant who is terrified to be in front of a crowd is not learning how to tie a splint, even if one is being tied on their own arm this very moment.

Voluntolds might be capable of completing the same tasks as a volunteer, but they are processing the experience very differently and this can lead to challenges in the bigger picture. With a little insight into their experience, you can be prepared for this and help to make the relationship more pleasant for everyone involved.

Partnerships with organizations who voluntell people to make the world a better place can be beneficial for everyone involved. An inmate from a local correctional facility performing community service is benefiting from social interaction, the development of useful skills, and belonging to a team. A student from a local high school who is looking to complete their required volunteer hours to graduate is benefiting from gaining experience that will be good on a resume, connections for helping to find employment, and mentorship. And your organization gets some free help!

Just remember that someone informed that they had to volunteer against their will is likely experiencing a higher stress level and that can make it more difficult for them to learn the role. It's not unusual for individuals who are completing community service hours as part of their sentencing to be mistaken for being surly, rude, withdrawn, difficult, or disengaged and the problem is usually chalked up to "they're just like that". Which is sad because the problem is more often rooted in the level of anxiety they are feeling. The more information you can provide about the nature of the task you are asking them to complete (it's okay, there are no polar bears) and the more you can make clear where to find help if they need it (there are other penguins here to show you the ropes), the less guarded they will be and the more quickly they can learn how to do the job you're asking to have done, and do it well.

4. ACKNOWLEDGE GIFTS OF TIME BIG AND SMALL

People don't volunteer time out of their lives. They volunteer out of their *margin*. The other commitments they have in their lives will determine how many hours they can make available to volunteer. For example, the volunteer who gives 20 hours a week might have nothing else to do other than eat and sleep. After volunteering they still have plenty of time on their hands. Giving you 20 hours didn't put them out too much. Another volunteer might give an hour and then it's six months before you see them again for another hour. That person might be working two jobs, have three kids, be recovering from a car accident and still have regular therapy appointments (with no car) and not only do they want to give you some of the limited time they have to call their own, but they worked hard to get to you. Volunteer passion and effort can't be measured in hours. Rather than conclude that volunteer hours are not worth tracking, the suggestion I'm making is simply be wary of awarding volunteers based on their hours. Someone who gave you four hours may have worked a whole lot harder to give it to you than someone who gave forty. Be sure to acknowledge and thank everyone in some way (meals and draws for prizes are great equalizers and we'll explore those under Gratitude). Cultivating the attitude of gratitude for all donations of time will help you to grab more volunteers when on the resource campaign trail because a lot of people are convinced they can't volunteer because they can't give *a lot* of time. Knowing that there are places where an hour or two of their time is still valued can be all that was needed to get them signed up!

5. TRY TO CREATE MARGIN FOR VOLUNTEERS

The last point highlighted that people don't give volunteer hours out of their lives, they give it out of their *margin*, the space left in their lives that isn't already filled with commitments. Many people feel harassed when asked to volunteer, even if they want to, only because they are already running on fumes and it feels like someone asking for one hour of time is asking for the only hour they have left. They have no margin for themselves, let alone any margin to give to someone else. (Side note: For anyone who is in that position I *highly* recommend that you learn more about stress reduction in order to gain practical tools for creating a more sustainable schedule and preserving your health before you burn out! Visiting www.stresswinner.com is a good place to start.)

Believe it or not, organizations looking for volunteers actually have an opportunity to help people create more margin in their lives rather than simply asking people to give out of what they have left! And if you can do that you have an even greater chance of getting people to sign up. Here is an example.

A student would like to learn more about politics and volunteer during a political campaign, however, they play soccer, take care of their little sister after school on Mondays and Thursdays, and are failing math so their parents signed them up for a math tutor on Wednesdays. Add in the rest of their homework and that busing to your site would take 45 minutes instead of the 10-minute drive it would otherwise be and they don't feel like they have any time left to give.

Your political campaign team may have an opportunity to help this student *create margin* so that they are able to contribute. There may be another volunteer living nearby and, if so, would his parents consider meeting the volunteer and approving a carpool? If he's able to come on Mondays and Thursdays, would his parents allow his younger sister to come help too? Would his parents consider letting him volunteer and work with the finance manager to develop his math skills in a real-life context rather than tutoring? Does he want to bring his homework with him? He can man the phone lines and when there are no calls he can work on his biology assignment. When we get to the gratitude chapter we'll take a look at what kind of impact asking the question "What can we do for you" can have for your organization. For now, just think about what creating margin for volunteering does for that student and then in turn for your organization.

That student posts on their social media that a political party is letting them work with money to learn math. Friends take note that a political party invested in their friend and want to know if they can get involved and volunteer too. Each of those students shares with their friends what they're learning about politics and the voting process. Word of mouth spreads throughout their school that there is a party investing in truly connecting with people their age. A whole new group of young voters head to the polls on election day and know who their party of choice is.

Can creating margin for volunteers get complicated? In the short term, yes, but I find more often than not when things get too complex that's our own darn fault. We're the ones making it more complicated than it needs to be. If someone throws you the line "we can't do that" you can hit them up with some George Bernard Shaw who said, "Those who say it can not be done should not interrupt those who are doing it." If something seems too complex to make happen then stop and ask if things can be made more simple (and hint, the answer is always yes).

Can creating margin for volunteers get messy? Absolutely. I'm not going to pretend like everything will work out all the time. Some experiments in creating margin will blow up in your face rather fantastically. But it's worth the risk for all the other times it works out wonderfully and the ripple effect goes out from that one volunteer, grabbing a larger group of people you wouldn't have been able to connect with otherwise.

6. NEVER TELL SOMEONE THAT GIVING MONEY IS A SIGN OF TRUE COMMITMENT

If you want to lose your volunteers, or utterly sour your relationship with them, tell them their time, knowledge and skills aren't good enough and you want their money. Organizations would never in a million years say it *that way,* and yet they do say it regularly.

Organizations write clauses in their contracts and agreements with Board and committee members, somewhere below the clause on appropriate conduct and above the clause about conflicts of interest, that members of these bodies will *donate to the institution in order to demonstrate leadership.*

Organizations approach their Board of Directors or committees to ask if they would consider putting money on the table for a matching campaign. *We want to show our donors that we are putting our money where our mouth is.*

Organizations encourage their volunteers to give money *to show that they actually believe in the organization.*

Organizations encourage their volunteers to *give big to show that they have skin in the game.*

Any of those look or sound familiar? I strongly recommend, if you want to move forward into the world of resource campaigning and all that it has to offer your organization, take the time to go through all your documents including contracts, agreements, and volunteer communications and *remove all of the statements above* if you find them in your literature. It's a horrible waste of a connection if you engage a volunteer only to have them read the fine print of some document they have to sign that's been in circulation for ten years which requires them to commit their money. In the privacy of their home office, while they read the documents you emailed them as part of the protocol for joining this committee, something deep inside them is broken and their relationship to you changes in an instant. And most organizations I encounter have no idea what kind of impact this is having. They just wonder why Board meetings seem to be so tense and why there is so much arguing around the upcoming fundraiser...

Just in case this is happening in your organization, please, stop asking your Board of Directors for money. It doesn't matter how wealthy they are or what additional resources they have access to. Don't ever expect that someone should give you more than their time if that is what they have offered you. They know where to find you if they have more resources they want to give and simply being aware of the challenges and needs of the organization is usually enough to trigger their interest in giving. But to be asked, even worse *told*, that more is needed from them because their time isn't enough is as good as spitting in their face.

7. BE CAREFUL WHEN ASKING FOR VOLUNTEERS TO ONLY ASK FOR THEIR *TIME*

Depending on what you are asking a volunteer to do there may be expenses associated with being able to accomplish that duty. For example, if you are asking for free first aid training you are actually asking for two resource categories. You are asking for time (a volunteer instructor who won't charge for their services) and for free specific items (training manuals, manikin lungs, gloves, and other one-use items required to teach the class). The instructor may be willing to volunteer, but if they give you the class for free they are also *paying* money for the materials to make it happen. Organizations will get the best response from volunteers if they ask them to provide quotes for any expenses associated with them giving of their time and skillset so that the organization can pay for them. This gives the volunteer the opportunity to choose if they also want to donate the materials, or if they want to bill for them. Having that option and making the choice, instead of the specific items being asked of them or assumed to be part of the deal, will build and protect long-term relationships with your volunteers.

Canadian Red Cross

First Aid, Water Safety, Disaster Management, International Operations, Respect Education, Home Care Services, and more!

The Canadian Red Cross is part of a global Red Cross movement whose mission is to mobilize the power of humanity, empowering human beings to help their fellow human beings. Guided by the 7 Fundamental Principles of humanity, impartiality, neutrality, independence, *voluntary service*, unity, and universality this organization looks at local and global needs and steps into the gaps to help.

Because human needs are so diverse any number of services have developed which creates a multitude of volunteer opportunities. The organization is large enough and the movement broad enough that literally, anyone can find a place to volunteer that resonates with their personal passions and they can do so within their home country or travel the globe.

The Red Cross currently has 20,000+ volunteers active in Canada alone!

To learn more visit:

Canadian Red Cross
www.redcross.ca

International Federation of the Red Cross (assists humanity during times of peace)
www.ifrc.org

International Committee of the Red Cross (assists humanity during times of war)
[caution, disturbing images]
www.icrc.org

12

MONEY

These relationships thrive when a person feels their money is providing benefit to someone whether the organization, the recipient of the organization's efforts or the donor themselves (ex. Good feelings or charitable tax deductions).

These relationships are *deeply injured* if you connect closely with the person for no other reason than to ask for money, or by asking for money too often.

MONEY

The base 17% (which you've always been getting when fundraising)

> These relationships thrive when a person feels their money is
> providing benefit to someone whether the organization, the
> recipient of the organization's efforts or the donor themselves
> (ex. Good feelings or charitable tax deductions).
>
> These relationships are *deeply injured* if you connect closely
> with the person for no other reason than to ask for money, or
> by asking for money too often.

The following suggestions can help to make sure your requests for money reflect the language of resource campaigning and are helping to build your donor community rather than fracture it into the classic 17/83 split fundraisers create. Use relationship-based language and you'll have the opportunity to receive from the 100% you connect with and get money from 17% of them.

1. AVOID USING SENTENCES THAT JUST ASK FOR MONEY

Share multiple resources you are looking for before asking the person if they are interested in contributing. If you ask for money and then wait for their response before providing other resource options there is a higher chance that the person will tune you out and excuse themselves before you get a chance to share any more. The reason is that they've been exposed to literally *thousands of fundraisers* by the time they get to you and they assume that's all there was to the interaction. The classic fundraising exchange:

Can we have some of your money? Yes? No? Okay. Have a nice day.

It's like autopilot. *Make sure autopilot doesn't kick in.* Make sure they know you are doing something different. Make sure they know there are more ways than handing over cash to support your organization in reaching its goals.

BAD: "Hello, we're an organization that helps college and university campuses create safe spaces for students who experience intense anxiety. Would you like to make a financial contribution to support our efforts? We have other resources we're looking for as well. Would you have any interest in volunteering? We're also collecting couch cushions with positive messages on them which can be commonly found in home decorating stores. If you'd like to donate any to our safe spaces initiative you can drop them off at this address."

GOOD: "Hello, we're an organization that helps college and university campuses create safe spaces for students who experience intense anxiety. We have three campuses we are currently supporting and are looking for funds to help expand our reach to more campuses, volunteers to help educate students and faculty about what it's like to experience an anxiety attack and how to help, and are also collecting decorative couch cushions with positive messages on them. Are you interested in any of the things I've mentioned so far or know of someone else who might be?"

By treating all of The 6 Key Resource Categories as equals, rather than money as the priority and the remaining resources as the sad leftovers you can ask for if you don't get money, then you're likely to get more of everything! Remember money comes in a couple of different forms and asking for funds will only get you a small portion of it.

2. KNOW EXACTLY WHAT YOUR ORGANIZATION NEEDS

The amount you say you need is going to create prompts for your donors' brains regarding how much to give. If you say you need $200, $2,000, or $200,000 it can make the difference between whether someone gives you a dollar, a twenty dollar bill, or cuts you a check for $500. Small needs often attract smaller donations. Big needs often attract bigger donations. Just saying you need money and hoping for the best outcome possible is not good communication and can cause you to seriously miss your mark.

3. BE CLEAR THAT CONNECTING WITH THE PERSON IS YOUR PRIORITY

Money causes people to do weird things. How weird? The term 'gold digger' is generally used to refer to someone who is willing to *fake a relationship*, possibly to the extent of a life-long commitment to someone, *just so they can have access to their money*. Some people don't even have the benefit of a good life with the person who wants their money. They get a rude shock after the wedding, finding out the loving relationship was a lie and that they were tricked into a commitment because of the size of their bank account. Gold diggers don't just go after the millionaires and billionaires. Their modus operandi is usually just to glob on to someone who has 'more'. People, in general, are wary of being taken advantage of, there are any number of false friends out there (wealthy individuals have probably been burned by a fundraising campaign manager or two in the past), so making clear that you value the person first and their contribution second can go a long way towards building lasting trust. And if people are not your priority, if you honestly just want their money because they have more than you, please go find a mountaintop somewhere to go be alone and sort yourself out. Your life is not working right now.

4. ALWAYS BE AVAILABLE TO RECEIVE BUT DO NOT ALWAYS ASK

This is one of the Universal Resource Campaign Principles, however, I'm highlighting it again here because fundraising practices will be trying to push their way back into your consciousness and practice. While you are blazing your resource campaign trail any number of fundraising resources are still going to be churned out and marketed to you, trying to tell you all the ways you can keep asking, asking, asking. Make sure your donor community knows where to find you if they want to give, but stay in touch with them for other reasons than asking.

If you have two adult children, one who writes home to tell you about their latest adventures, sends you pictures, and asks how you are doing and another who writes you from time to time with a few sentences that always lead to the words 'need money', you'll probably have a better relationship with the first and dread to some degree hearing from the second. You want the relationship with the second to be better, but that's not entirely in your control. The only person you have any control over is you and so while you do your best, you hope that kid wakes up and starts trying to genuinely connect and not just ask, ask, ask.

Don't let your organization become the second kid. Reach out to just talk or to give back and make sure donors always know how to reach you. You'll find that over time, with the relationship invested in, some resources will be offered without your having to ask and when you do ask the request will be positively received.

Salvation Army

Christmas Campaign

The Salvation Army has a multitude of thrift store locations where people can drop off donations of all kinds at almost any time. The general approach is that if you have something you would like to donate, you know where to find them (or can find out pretty quickly).

However, when Christmas rolls around a larger volunteer team is gathered to sit in malls, in grocery stores, on street corners, and other high foot traffic areas next to a container in order to collect cash donations. They often ring bells to attract attention and attempt to greet and directly connect with as many people walking by as possible, wishing them a Merry Christmas and a happy holiday season. They *receive* year round. They *ask* at Christmas time.

The Salvation Army Christmas Campaign is now considered a staple of the holiday season. Is it Christmas time? Then it's time to see the Salvation Army volunteer sitting in the foyer of the local grocery store. The overall response from the community is both positive and financially beneficial to the organization.

Learn more:

https://www.salvationarmy.ca/

13

CONNECTIONS

These relationships thrive when a Connector can say, "I know just the person you're looking for," and has an opportunity to put you in touch with them.

These relationships are *deeply injured* when the Connector is told you'd like to connect with anyone and everyone they know. This communicates to them I don't care about you or the people you know, I just want your contact list. Connectors enjoy making specific connections that are beneficial to both parties and don't like having their connections taken advantage of for impersonal gain.

These relationships thrive when a donor can say, "I know just the person you're looking for," and has an opportunity to put you in touch with them.

These relationships are *deeply injured* when the donor is told you'd like to connect with anyone and everyone they know. This communicates to them *I don't care about you or the people you know, I just want your contact list.* These donors enjoy making *specific* connections that are beneficial to both parties and don't like having their connections taken advantage of for impersonal gain.

When a donor is triggered into Connection mode it means you've said something that has made them excited to share with someone else. They're not interested in sharing with everyone. Instead, a specific person has been brought to mind and they see enough benefit to you connecting with them that they are willing to gift you with necessary contact information or will pass your information on so the person can contact you. If someone lights up and says you should connect with so-and-so, that's a valuable connection to make! The fact that you can say, "I was speaking with _____ who recommended I contact you and gave me your information…" usually gives you an automatic foot in the door. You're not a stranger calling (which lots of people hate). You are a connection of a connection. That usually makes your request for help worth consideration.

Everyone at multiple points in their lives goes into Connection mode when asked for help, but this particular donor category has some connecting rockstars hiding in it.

Everyone has connections, but some people are Connectors. Everyone has a network of some kind, but Connectors can point with laser precision to the exact person who will be the most benefit to call up. They have an uncanny ability to recall random snippets from past conversations and to see how two different people's thoughts, resources, or needs could converge for something bigger to happen. They are the ones who know someone getting rid of baby clothes and also know exactly whose kid could benefit from them. They are the ones who hear about someone's legal troubles and remember talking to a law student ten years ago studying that exact subject who must be an experienced lawyer by now and will help connect the two.

They are the ones who, if you're looking for someone with a specific skill set, probably know a guy. And if they don't, then they know a guy who knows a guy!

Connectors have an additional quirk in that they aren't aware there is anything particularly remarkable about their memories, or their tendency to keep people on their radars. To them, it's natural and many assume that everyone does this. But not everyone does. Only a small handful. So when you connect with a Connector, consider that a huge blessing because the resources they have to offer you are mighty.

What they are aware of is that their connections are precious to them and valuable to others, and if someone comes sniffing around wanting access to everyone they know then that person is not to be trusted.

Don't ask Connectors for access to all of their contacts. If you end up in the bad books of a Connector that will have long-term consequences because they will *remember*. The results can include not pointing people in your direction if they suspect you'll give other people trouble. Even worse, if they think poorly of you and come across someone else dealing on your level they might see you as a perfect fit for each other and be willing to match you up. If you're not held in high esteem by a Connector they can end up sending trouble your way.

When a Connector gives you a name and phone number, or a promise to write an introductory email tomorrow, and does not give to your organization in any other way, fundraising mentality says you failed to get money, but at least you got more contacts. Resource campaigning acknowledges the contact information you've been given and the resulting connection as a valuable gift in and of itself because it's not a random name from a phone book where you are starting from scratch. Remember that resource campaigning knows you need to connect with people, not just contact them, and when you connect with someone you are guaranteed to receive something from one of The 6 Key Resource Categories. When a Connector *connects* you that's a guaranteed gift of some kind. Great!

Note: Everyone has the capacity to respond from any of The 6 Key Resource Categories depending on who is asking them for resources at the time. However, the Connector's gift of connections is also rooted in an innate ability. This means they are more likely to give in this way more often. Know who your Connectors are!!!

Here are a few additional principles to keep in mind to help you make the most of this resource category:

1. PEOPLE WHO VOLUNTEER TO CONNECT AND THOSE GIFTING CONNECTIONS ARE NOT THE SAME THING

It's easy to walk past Connections donors and *Connectors* without realizing it if you don't know what you're looking for. One of the reasons they don't necessarily stand out from the crowd is because there are plenty of people who will volunteer to connect you with others. They'll share your post on Facebook, they'll tell their friends about your upcoming event, forward your e-newsletter if you ask them to, and tell the world! But people who simply pass on the message are not Connections donors or Connectors. They fall into your volunteer category. They are giving their time to take action to help you out, doing what you asked them to do, pass it on. Connections donors and Connectors *are not interested in passing on messages*. They are interested in *connecting people*. Tune your radar to recognize individuals who have someone specific in mind, or who love connecting people, not just spreading the word, and you'll have a better sense of who the Connections donors and Connectors are in your donor community.

2. DON'T ASK CONNECTORS TO PASS ON MESSAGES TO EVERYONE THEY KNOW

If you ask, lots of people will do this, but not your Connectors! Your Connectors will share messages with *the contacts they believe are most likely to resonate with the message you're sending out*. Asking a Connector to send your materials on to everyone they know is like asking them to connect with a few people they know and unnecessarily bother the rest. They're not going to do it.

So watch your wording and where you place requests for messages to be passed on *carefully*. In any sections where you are asking for connections, asking Connections donors and Connectors to send your message on to anyone they can think of *who would be interested* is more likely to trigger their interest in helping. Save statements like "please share on Facebook" or "forward to your friends" for the footer or put it in your volunteering section. Putting any statements in text geared towards Connections donors and Connectors regarding passing messages on to anyone and everyone is likely to trigger their distrust that you just want access to their contact list, causing them to click 'delete'.

3. BE SPECIFIC ABOUT WHO YOU ARE TRYING TO CONNECT WITH!

People's brains fire up when you start giving details. Imagine a database that is constantly cross-referencing information as it is entered. You said you're a performer. *Processing.* You perform in children's theatre productions? *Narrowing results.* You perform for the purpose of sharing anti-bullying messages and equipping youth to get help if they need it? *Narrowing results.* And you're looking for more schools to connect with where you could perform? *Bing!* I was just talking to Carol three months ago and she was saying that bullying is a real problem in her classroom. Let me get you her number...

To say you are 'looking for people' is a blank statement. Asking Google to find you 'something' doesn't really get you fantastic search results. When in doubt, treat your Connections donors like Google. The more specific you can be, the better chances you have of getting a spot-on response to your query.

We are looking to connect with people in the Greater Toronto region who love walking dogs.

We are looking to connect with people who have experienced loss as the result of impaired driving who are passionate about preventing similar losses for other families.

We are looking to connect with a real estate lawyer who specializes in, and has experience with, industrial properties, preferably based in Victoria, British Columbia.

It might seem intuitive at first that to ask for more broad categories of people will result in getting more connections, but that's old fundraising mentality around building your list of contacts popping up. More is better! Nope. When looking for connections remember that narrowing the field will actually give you greater results for meeting your specific needs!

The Trevor Project

Saving Young LGTBQ Lives

The Trevor Project summarizes themselves as following on their website:

The Trevor Project is the leading national organization providing crisis intervention and suicide prevention services to lesbian, gay, bisexual, transgender and questioning (LGBTQ) young people ages 13-24.

They are very specific about the population they are trying to reach and their reason for trying to reach them. If someone knows an LGBTQ youth or young adult who is in distress and needs support they can point them in the direction of Trevor.

The Trevor Project is also looking to connect with volunteers who want to end suicide for LGBTQ young people. They are not simply interested in ending suicide, which any number of organizations are working towards, but are aiming to end suicide for a very specific population with more specific challenges and needs.

As the result of their clarity regarding who they are looking for any number of people have been connected with this lifesaving organization. There is every reason to believe that The Trevor Project will continue to expand its outreach and its team by leaps and bounds in the coming years.

Learn more:

https://www.thetrevorproject.org

14

GRATITUDE

These relationships thrive when your donor community sees that you value their contribution and give something valuable back.

These relationships are *deeply injured* if the person receives a gift of crap or if it becomes clear that your organization only takes.

GRATITUDE (+17%)

> These relationships thrive when your donor community sees that you value their contribution and give something valuable back.
>
> These relationships are *deeply injured* if the person receives a gift of crap or if it becomes clear that your organization only takes.

Gratitude is the least tangible of The 6 Key Resource Categories, but the better you understand it the more clearly you can see it has equal value and equal importance alongside the other five resource categories.

Gratitude is the gift of goodwill and good thoughts which translates into supportive speech and actions when the opportunity presents itself.

What does that look like in real life? They may never purchase your services, give you specific items, volunteer, give you funds, or connect you with anyone, but if they see that someone put graffiti on your sign they'll be the ones to wash it off before you even knew you'd been spray painted.

They are the ones who overhear a lost couple at the gas station trying to figure out where you are and give them directions.

They're the ones who come along after your event and pick up the stray bits of garbage blowing around so that no one in the community complains or thinks less of you.

The reality is that most of the things your Gratitude donors give you you'll never know about. But that doesn't make their gifts and actions any less valuable. And if as part of your resource campaigning you know that you left that person's presence with nothing more than having had a positive interaction and making a connection, you didn't actually leave with nothing. You just encountered one of your Gratitude donors. Consider that connection a success.

Their gratitude is the result of being thankful that you are a part of their community. To some degree, we all have a sense that we can't fix the world on our own. There are too many problems, our own personal resources don't stretch that far, and if we're honest then there are some issues that we know are issues, but we just don't care. Thank goodness there is someone else out there with a heart for that who is taking care of it!

Organizations seem to garner the most gratitude when they invest in building good relationships with their *external* community (the broader human context they happen to operate in whether their town, province, country or the world depending on the size and scope of their organization) and their *internal* community (staff and volunteers).

Starting with your external community, gratitude is fostered first by just saying why you exist and what you do. People are going to be grateful that you are caring for the corner of the world that you are because it means that they don't have to do it! It is then further fostered when you say thank you to your community and give something to them.

What you give to your community is important because in order to foster gratitude it ultimately has to be about them and not about you. When an animal shelter hosts a dog show with entry fees and prizes and the proceeds go to the animal shelter, well then, that's about the animal shelter! But when an animal shelter hosts a skateboarding event for youth for the sheer joy of giving a great experience to a community where there is a strong skateboarding population, that is about the community. This kind of event says *we're glad you're a part of our community* which in turn fosters a sense of gratitude, people being grateful that you're a part of their community too.

What you give to your internal community matters because these individuals are giving to you on a regular basis. Many organizations make the mistake of thinking their staff are paid to be there so they aren't really 'giving' and therefore there should be no expectation of the organization giving them anything more than their due wages. The reality is that many people sacrifice taking on jobs with higher paying salaries in order to do something they love and to dedicate their lives to a cause they are passionate about. That lower pay can mean they've given up any number of things such as a more comfortable apartment, a new winter coat to replace their current one which is falling apart, nicer vacations, and more. I'm not talking about someone giving up living in a five-bedroom house in order to just live in a four-bedroom house, or someone settling for a new Honda Civic instead of a Ferrari. I'm talking about people living in dingy fixer-uppers, people who have sewn their coat sleeve back on at the shoulder twice this winter, and people who have settled for keeping their dream of visiting Scotland a dream because they've chosen to take a job with lower pay that gives them the satisfaction of doing something they love.

Early in my career I had people regularly commenting in the Winter about my footwear. I did not have appropriate boots on to keep my feet warm considering the temperature and the depth of the snow. The problem was that despite having a career that took me outside on a regular basis I didn't have the money to buy boots. I had chosen for the time to accept lower pay in order to be able to do something I *loved* and if that meant having cold feet for a bit I could deal with that.

There is something to be said for the benefits of living simply and knowing how to live on a tighter budget, but it is foolish for an organization to assume that because they are paying someone to perform a service that that person is not 'giving' their time or resources. Coming to understand and acknowledge just how much they are giving, or giving up while being paid, will help your organization to better say 'thank you' and to foster ongoing good things for everyone involved.

Whether you are fostering gratitude within your external community or your internal community the following principles will help you out:

1. WHEN IN DOUBT, HELP OUT

If the idea of collecting gratitude as a gift for your organization is a new concept that you're working with then here's a great place to get started. When in doubt, help out. The simple question, "how can I/we help you" will open up all sorts of opportunities. People *love* being asked this question because, even if they don't need help with anything, they value that you asked! And if they did need help they love that someone offered and made their lives a little easier.

I mentioned earlier that asking someone if they need help can feel intimidating because it feels like handing someone a blank check. What will they ask for? What am I getting myself in to? But most people will either say they don't need anything, ask you for help in the form of information, or have a very reasonable request that will take a small amount of time and effort to assist with. The effort invested gives a much higher return in gratitude.

If you would feel more confident knowing the exact parameters of an offer rather than taking the 'blank check' approach you can always connect directly with people whose needs you are already familiar with. Is there an elderly couple on your road who has trouble shovelling their driveway during the Winter? Offer to take turns as staff to clear their drive for them when needed. Is there a school that lost a number of library books to a leaking roof? Do a book collection to help replace their resources. Do you have a staff member who has 5000 envelopes to stuff? Put together a team of people and have an envelope stuffing party with music and some great coffee.

One of my greatest memories from my time working with a camping and outdoor education facility is the day our team did a work project at a local horse farm. The owner offered riding lessons to youth and took in foster animals when a farm animal was seized because of abuse. She was someone we were thankful to have as part of our community and so we asked her if there was anything we could do to help her. It turned out that she had been trying for years to open up a second larger practice ring for her students, but the space was full of rocks which made it unusable because it could hurt the horses' ankles. She had been trying to clear the field, but never had enough time on her hands to properly make a dent and get any forward momentum. She was one person trying to get the job done. We were a team of fifteen.

A date was set and on that morning we packed into three cars, showed up ready to get dirty and got to work. It was a great day. It was a great bonding experiencing for our team and set us up to have a great dynamic going into the next season of work. It was a day full of memories including riding in wheelbarrows, getting to play with the bunnies in the barn during our lunch break, and one particularly memorable battle of man-versus-rock when three of the gentlemen realized one of the boulders they were trying to pick up was just the tip of the iceberg. They gave up a portion of their lunch to haul that thing out of the ground with the tractor and you should have heard the cheering and seen their faces when they were victorious. We had a short snowball fight with dried manure (don't ask) and had an amazing day that was talked about for weeks afterwards.

When in doubt, help out. Clean-up and work projects are particularly great when-in-doubt options for fostering gratitude both within your external and internal communities.

2. THE VALUE OF A GIFT COMMUNICATES HOW MUCH YOU VALUE THE RECIPIENT

When you give gifts, the value of the gift will communicate how much you value your donor community. One of the worst things an organization can do is just give something for the sake of giving something. I have seen any number of tacky knick-knacks with an organization's logo emblazoned on it exchange hands in the name of thanking people for their time and efforts.

The organizations had no idea how much they just insulted their community or damaged their relationship with them.

This theme has popped up a couple of times now so we'll hammer it home now. Crap should never have a place in your organization. Small and affordable things can still be quality. It is worth the effort to find these items so that you communicate value to your community rather than communicating they mean about as much to you as this cheap plastic ball-point pen and fridge magnet.

If you don't have a large budget for this sort of thing, the point isn't to spend a lot of money. If you can get everyone a company car that's pretty awesome, but if all you can afford to do is upgrade the coffee station with a better machine and some better coffee for everyone to enjoy, that goes a long way.

3. IT'S BETTER TO GIVE ONE PERSON A VALUABLE GIFT THAN GIVE EVERYONE CRAP

Many organizations sincerely believe they need to hand out pens and fridge magnets with their logo and contact information on it so that people will remember them and get in touch. That idea was a sales tactic used by the companies making the pens and fridge magnets. Useless or semi-useless crap is not what is going to get people calling you. These days, if you want to be remembered, *be memorable*. If someone needs to find your contact information they'll use Google.

I don't know where the idea came from, but there is also a pervasive belief that if you're going to give something to someone then you have to give something to everyone. No. No, you don't. And if that means you diluted your budget from being able to purchase one really nice gift to only being able to afford crap for everyone, you've shot yourself in the foot. Only have $200 for thank you gifts and 20 people on your team? Well, $10 each will let you get each of them a cheap hat. Or you can do a draw for one gift of $200 cash. Which one would you want?

Even when people don't win they rarely walk away upset that their company didn't give them anything. Instead, they marvel at being connected to an organization that *would be willing to give them something that nice*.

As well, buying one really nice thing for one person doesn't tend to make other people upset, but instead leads to them being happy for someone else. The key to making this work is to make sure your parameters for giving one person a nice gift and nothing to the others is based on defined criteria or a random draw, never subjective choices.

What that means is that if the gift of a $500 gift card will go to the person who received the highest overall customer satisfaction rating on the evaluation forms throughout the year, that's a measurable parameter and not open to interpretation. If the gift will go to the person whose name is drawn out of this hat then everyone has a fair chance. But if the gift will go to the most positive person who brought the most energy to the team this year… that is up for interpretation and can lead to some disgruntled chatter later between the people who know Susie from accounting is not always little miss sunshine and know Greg is quiet but a huge encouragement to the team.

Draws, in particular, are great equalizers and if people know that simply continuing to be a part of the internal or external community means that they have a shot at receiving a really nice gift, that can build and sustain a sense of gratitude in everyone for a very long time.

4. IF YOU'RE GOING TO GIVE THE GIFT OF GRATITUDE, GET IT RIGHT!

It's gala dinner night! The night your organization says thank you to its community, staff and volunteers, handing out certificates of recognition to its team members and scholarships to the community it serves. The Lifetime Achievement Award goes to Ben Friesen who has been a part of your organization for 27 years (actually it's 28). The Honours Award for going the extra mile as a volunteer goes to Anna Pelkin (whose last name should have been spelled Pelken). Congratulations to Kai Yu-Ning, the recipient of the Future Leaders Scholarship, who has overcome adversity with cerebral palsy and will be attending the University of Waterloo to pursue his studies in the sciences (a very vague statement, but you forgot he's studying criminal psychology and that's a science…). For all the sparkle and grandeur of the evening here are some likely outcomes to anticipate. Ben has a nagging question in the back of his head about how accurate the volunteer records are which has lessened his confidence in the organization he has dedicated so much of his life to. Anna was going to show off her certificate proudly but decides instead to put it in a drawer because anyone who knows how to spell her name properly will ask questions and looking at the mistake makes her feel a bit sad. Kai is wondering if he's a publicity stunt and if the only reason he was given an award was so you could have your picture taken shaking the hands of someone with cerebral palsy. This evening has not gone well.

If you are going to spell someone's name, spell it right. If you're going to say how long they've been with you, get it right. If you're going to share what they are studying, where they are going next, how many kids they have, what condition they've overcome, what pets they have, anything, Get It Right. A little slip up might not seem like a big deal, but the message it ultimately communicates is that you weren't listening or don't care. At best people assume you are busy and have a lot to keep track of so mistakes are going to happen. At worst they feel overlooked or used and disengage from your organization. Check. Double check. Triple check if you have to. Just get it right.

A NOTE ON MEALS

Meals together are an incredibly powerful way of bringing your community together. A great basic rule for bonding people together is, "When in doubt, break bread!" Meals are also a great equalizer when you are trying to say thank you for contributions outwardly big and small without knowing how much it actually cost someone behind the scenes to give (as discussed earlier in Specific Items and Volunteering).

In an age where people's food needs can be so diverse due to allergies, intolerances, faith, or deeply held principles it is wise to learn before a meal if there is anything that the people attending can not eat. Once you know, get it right! Being intentional and very careful about food needs might shape your overall menu, change how you serve the meal, or result in creating some additional side meals that meet the needs of very specific people.

It is worth every ounce of effort put into accommodating these needs because food has a unique role in our existence as human beings and has the power to create a sense of bonding or isolation. Having even one person excuse themselves from a meal because they are afraid of or averse to the food can harm a relationship. At the very least it is a missed opportunity.

Don't worry about making everyone happy with the menu. It would be near impossible to accommodate every food preference or fad diet that is represented somewhere within your team. The main focus is making sure that a meal is not life-threatening, will not cause physical pain later, and does not violate one's faith or deeply held principle. If a caterer is not able to accommodate all the needs then a potluck can be a great way to go. This allows everyone to bring a

QUICK GUIDE TO GRATITUDE GIFT GIVING

Here are some examples of good gifts and crap to establish some filters for
gift giving:

GOOD

- Cash
- Event tickets or venue passes (make sure they can go with a friend)
- Travel voucher or all-expenses-paid vacation (a gift should never cost
  the person)
- Large gift card ($25 bare minimum)
- Free services from your organization
- Thoughtful quality items (ex. Tablet, camping tent, espresso machine,
  etc)
- Quality clothing and accessories (ex. Hoodie, rain jacket, etc)
- High-quality plaque or framed quality certificate with the person's
  correct information

CRAP

- Pens (even the nice ones, the only value is if the pen has greater
  meaning because of specific traditions in your organization or
  profession or if the person has stated they would like a really nice pen)
- Small candies (food gifts in general, only buy a treat if you know that is
  exactly what they like. If they like mint chocolate find out *exactly*
  which mint chocolate they enjoy - never guess or substitute!)
- Mugs
- Fridge magnets
- Stress balls
- Knick-knacks
- Cheap clothing and accessories (ex. Cheap hats, cheap pins, etc)
- Common printer-paper certificates (remember people are tactile, get
  the nice paper!)
- Plaques or certificates with mistakes

IS A T-SHIRT A GOOD GIFT OR CRAP?

T-shirts are one of the most common gifts given. The following four filters will help determine if the shirt you are thinking of would be a good gift and a good use of your resources, or crap and a waste of your resources (and damaging to your connections):

1. Is the shirt made of quality material that won't notably shrink, *feels good* to the touch, and *breathes*?

2. Is the shirt a good design, flattering to the majority of body types, and long to accommodate various heights?

3. Is the design being printed on the shirt high quality, reflecting current or classic fashion trends? Is this something people will *want* to wear?

4. Is the shirt the right size for the person it's being given to? (There's zero point giving it to them if it doesn't fit)

If it checks all these boxes you're good to go. What a great gift! If even one question gets a 'no' then keep shopping around until you find a shirt that meets all the criteria.

The reality is that I don't know of any.

What non-profit organization do you know of that says 'thank you' in a way that shows they value their external and internal communities and that does not waste *any* resources purchasing, producing, or handing out crap?

Submit your suggestion!

You can go to the Facebook group Resource Campaign Community and share any organizations you can think of so that other members of the group can learn from their example!

15

TRANSITIONAL
CHANGE

Whatever the size of your endeavour, however much change you're looking to make, however fast or slow you're looking to make it, the following tools and questions can help you out. Look for something that resonates with you, something that sparks your interest and a sense of 'yes, we can start there' and get going!

TRANSITIONAL CHANGE

It's time to bundle all the concepts together!

However, I don't know if you are trying to raise $200 to pay for gas to get to a sports tournament one city over or if you're trying to raise millions of dollars for a global-wide effort.

I don't know if you're looking to dive head first into resource campaigning or if you have such a large and complex operation that transitioning will need to be a slow turning of the ship to a new heading.

Whatever the size of your endeavour, however much change you're looking to make, however fast or slow you're looking to make it, the following tools and questions can help you out. Look for something that resonates with you, something that sparks your interest and a sense of 'yes, we can start there' and get going!

BASIC BRAINSTORMING

Here is a simple and *great* way to get started. Just brainstorm what needs and wants you or your organization have now that you could start asking for immediately.

On the following two pages are sample brainstorming pages for an individual trying to raise personal support and a brainstorming page for an organization. Feel free to check them out for inspiration or skip those pages to go right into brainstorming what resources you're looking for!

BRAINSTORMING PAGE FOR INDIVIDUAL SUPPORT (SAMPLE)

[This individual is trying to gather resources in order to take a year off from work to go assist with disaster relief overseas.]

Purchased Services/Products
What do I offer that I'm trying to find more people to pay for?

I'm going to offer 5 workshops on disaster preparedness over the next three months, showing people how to protect their homes and create an emergency survival kit. $50 per person with proceeds helping to fund my trip. Trying to get 10 people minimum for each workshop.

Specific Items
What things am I looking for to meet my needs? What would be nice to have?

- *I need a new travel backpack, my old one won't survive another year.*
- *Mosquito net*
- *Sleeping bag for warm climate (I only have one for winter)*
- *Steel-plate and toe boots for walking on dangerous surfaces with sharp objects*
- *Water purification tablets*
- *Plane ticket there! It's expensive to get there!*
- *Plane ticket home! I would kind of like to come back home again…*
- *Food rations for emergency back up for myself and to share*
- *Medical supplies (what could I bring with me that could help?)*

Volunteering
Are there any tasks I need completed and would benefit from having help with?

I need help getting to the photo centre to get pictures to renew my passport. I can find someone to give me a ride. My washing machine is broken and leaking everywhere. If I can find someone to volunteer to fix it I can put the money I would have spent on repairs into my trip.

Money
Do I have any needs that can only be met through funds? What are they?
What is my total current need for funds?

*The reality is that I will need to have cash when I travel. I can't rely on credit
cards or debit in disaster zones. It would be wise to have $2000 cash for the trip.
I don't know what my needs will be, but I'll be prepared if something comes up.
I have my own money I am prepared to use, but if people give me money for the
trip then I can channel my funds into buying some of the other things I need or
buying more disaster supplies to bring with me.*

Connections
Are there any people or populations I'm hoping to specifically connect
with?

*I want to find a reliable person, possibly a bit down on their luck right now, who
would be interested in renting my apartment while I'm gone. They would be
responsible for their bills, but I'll cut them a deal on rent if they will take good
care of the place for me while I'm away.*

Gratitude
What can I do to simply give back to my donor community without asking
anything in return?

*I'll make each of my donors a small picture book of my time overseas when I get
back so they can see what their support achieved. I'll have them properly printed
with that photobook company my sister always gets her stuff done at so I know it
will be high quality. I can invite them to dinner and give as many of them their
photo books in person as possible. It will be nice to see everyone when I get back!*

WHAT RESOURCES AM I LOOKING FOR?
BRAINSTORMING EXERCISE FOR INDIVIDUALS

Purchased Services/Products
What do I offer that I'm trying to find more people to pay for?

Specific Items
What things am I looking for to meet my needs? What would be nice to have?

Volunteering
Are there any tasks I need completed and would benefit from having help with?

Money
Do I have any needs that can only be met through funds? What are they? What is my total current need for funds?

Connections
Are there any people or populations I'm hoping to specifically connect with?

Gratitude
What can I do to simply give back to my donor community without asking anything in return?

BRAINSTORMING PAGE FOR ORGANIZATION (SAMPLE)

[This camp which provides free Summer programs to children with special needs is trying to gather resources in order to increase revenue and make use of their property year-round, not just in the Summer.]

Purchased Services/Products
What do we offer that we are trying to find more people to pay for?

The property is usually closed during the Winter. This year we're looking to take out three groups for a Winter Camping experience so we can bring in more revenue to support our Summer programs (and make good use of the property. Seriously, it just sits there for 8 months out of the year.) The buildings aren't winterized so this will simply be an experience of living on the land during the Winter! The guided experience will be three days in total and include building and sleeping in quinces (or tents if the weather doesn't cooperate), campfire cookouts, snowshoeing, and other Winter fun (maybe some history about how people survive the Winter in various cultures). $250 per person, $600 per family, or $2000 for a group of up to 10. We can take up to 30 people out on a trip at a time.

Specific Items
What things are we looking for to meet our needs? What would be nice to have?

- *Five winter sleeping bags (someone always shows up with the wrong kind of sleeping bag for this kind of thing).*
- *Four travel snow shovels (saw some awesome fold up ones at the store!!!)*
- *Four more camping tents*
- *Fuel canisters for the cook stove. Can't have enough of those.*
- *1 winter camping tent with stove. We can use this to dry off wet gear and use it as an emergency shelter if someone is becoming hypothermic.*
- *Awesome food! Let's hit up M&M Meat shop and get a ton of finger foods for being able to snack while bigger meals are cooking. He who controls the food controls the troops! If anyone is feeling cold and miserable then having good food will lift their spirits.*
- *Should have lots of coffee, tea, and hot chocolate. Marshmallows for the kids for sure!*
- *Camping mugs (30)*

- *As many pairs of snowshoes as we can get our hands on. Let's start by asking for 30!*
- *Toboggans (no plastic! We need at least 10 wooden toboggans that can take a beating so we can haul all of our gear to the campsite!)*

Volunteering
Are there any tasks we need completed and would benefit from having help with?

We have two tents that could work but need repairs and it's a special seam. Who can we find that could do the repairs and make sure the seams stay waterproof? That would save us from having to replace the tents!

Maybe we could find a student willing to volunteer on one or more of the trips? It would reduce the number of paid staff we need to run the trips so a bit more money could go into our Summer programs and it would be a great experience for anyone hoping to go into Outdoor Education. Maybe contact the university that offers the OE program nearby and see if they have anyone interested?

Money
Do we have any needs that can only be met through funds? What are they? What is our total current need for funds?

If no one meets our needs for resources in other ways and we have to pay for everything then it's going to cost us $12,879.00 to get this up and running. Once we have the resources in hand it won't cost anywhere near that to keep the Winter program running. Woohoo! The only thing we need to pay money for is the staff which is $2,100.00 of that total. So we'd love at least that much in funds.

Connections
Are there any people or populations we're hoping to specifically connect with?

We need to find people who love Winter camping or are adventurous enough to try!!! Would love to find families so parents and kids can enjoy it together. Maybe ask local high schools (future OE students? Any high schools nearby offering outdoor programs. Schools may be interested in Winter field trips?).

Gratitude
What can we do to simply give back to our donor community without asking anything in return?

We could do a thank-you lunch and canoe outing in the Summer. It would be a chance for us to spoil them with some good food (we can show off our signature campfire bannock donuts!!!) and let them see the camp when the kids get here in the Summer so they can see the bigger picture of what they helped to make possible. We can just spoil them for the afternoon in appreciation for their support.

Maybe we could offer to do a birthday party for two kids who live in our region (some parameters would have to be established). We could do a draw for two birthday parties where two of our staff bring the camp to them for two hours. Run some games and activities. All for free. Just a thanks to our community and our way of giving back somehow. Just need to figure out how to let people know about the draw so they can submit their names.

The Johnsons on the property next to ours had a tree come down on their fence at the end of last Summer. If that section is still busted when we get out there we could do a group work project to repair it. With 15 or more people we could have it fixed in less than 2 hours. Could make for a fun team challenge.

WHAT RESOURCES ARE WE LOOKING FOR?
BRAINSTORMING EXERCISE FOR ORGANIZATIONS

Purchased Services/Products
What do we offer that we're trying to find more people to pay for?

Specific Items
What things are we looking for to meet our needs? What would be nice to have?

Volunteering
Are there any tasks we need completed and would benefit from having help with?

Money
Do we have any needs that can only be met through funds? What are they? What is our total current need for funds?

Connections
Are there any people or populations we're hoping to specifically connect with?

Gratitude
What can we do to simply give back to our donor community without asking anything in return?

1. Who in our broader team needs to sit down at the same table to talk about resource campaigning for our organization?

    Who is in charge of:

    (I) Finances

    (II) Fundraising

    (III) Human Resources

    (IV) Volunteer recruitment

    (V) Property management

    (VI) Inventory management

    (VII) Product delivery or program services

    (VIII) Communications

    (IX) Events

2. How can we collect insight from *everyone* in our organization regarding the needs they see for our survival and for our ability to reach further?

    (I) How can we ensure that as needs and wants surface within our team that they can make them known?

(II) How can we make sure we include this broader picture of our team's needs and wants in our campaign?

3. What tool(s) do we want to use to make our complete current list of wants and needs available to the public? Do we want to use a blog, Facebook page, website, bulletin board, a sheet of paper, etc?

4. Who is going to be responsible for keeping this shopping list of needs and wants up to date?

5. Are *all* of our communications covering all of the bases?

(I) Do all of our communications reflect the resources we are looking for from The 6 Key Resource Categories?

(II) Are we making sure that there are *zero* sentences that just ask for money?

(III) Are we trying to highlight each need equally instead of making it sound like funds are the priority?

6. In our social media where there is limited space to write, are we rotating our messages that we regularly cycle through and cover all of The 6 Key Resource Categories?

7. Are there any old social media posts we could benefit from deleting so people aren't confused and we can move forward with our resource campaign and relationship-based communications?

8. Are we sharing both our triumphs and our challenges? Are we being honest when things aren't going well?

(I) How can we build trust with our donors through communication of both the good things and the bad things happening for our organization?

9. Have we hired/trained anyone on our team to 'schmooze' on behalf of our organization?

(I) What can we do to change our mentality and set them up for being genuine and authentic when representing us?

10. Volunteering is one of The 6 Key Resource Categories. Do we currently invite people to join us?

(I) Would we know what to do if someone wanted to work with us?

(II) How can we incorporate volunteers into our team?

11. Do we have a legacy fund?

    (I) Are we using it as a fundraising tool (causing a 17/83 split of our donor community) or as a resource campaign tool (engaging all 100%), communicating all the other needs we have for resources at the same time we share we have a legacy fund?

12. Do we have any references to legacy funds and leaving us things when you die tucked away in our literature or social media that need to be updated?

    (I) Do we have any documents we need to update or posts that would benefit from being edited or deleted?

13. What scripts or suggested conversation starters do we want to provide our team with in order to support their ability to connect with more people and make sure they are covering all of The 6 Key Resource Categories?

14. Do we communicate clearly to donors exactly how our campaigns are going?

  (I) Do we provide regular updates and let people know when we've reached our goals or fallen short?

  (II) Is there any way we could improve that communication?

15. How often do we ask our donor community for resources?

(I)   Are our asking periods reasonably spread out?

(II) Do we have times of just connecting in between each period of asking?

(III) What can we do to just connect with our donor community without any asking included at all?

16. How much money are we asking for?

(I)   What are we planning on using that money for?

(II) Could any of those things be asked for in the shape of another resource category instead (ex. volunteering or the gift of specific items)?

17. Do we actually know exactly how much our organization needs?

(I) Do we have any literature that suggests "more is better" that needs to be updated or removed from circulation?

(II) What do we need to do to get exact numbers and communicate those numbers to our team and donor community?

18. How can we show our donors that we want to connect with them as *people* and not just get their resources?

(I) How can we show that we are listening and care about them personally?

19. How can we let our donor community know that we are available to receive any time of the year, even when we're not actively asking?

(I) If people want to give at times when we're not actively asking, have we made clear where to send those resources to?

20. Are there any tasks being completed by a paid team member that could instead be completed by a volunteer?

21. Are there any services we are paying for that we could try and find a volunteer to provide?

22. How clear are our volunteer position descriptions?

    (I) Have we provided as much information as possible to reduce applicant anxiety as much as possible?

    (II) Have we covered all the bases of:
- Who are you looking for
- What do you need this person to do
- Why is this person needed
- Where will they need to go to do this task
- When do they need to be there
- How do they get started

23. Are there any organizations we can partner with who have individuals requiring volunteer hours (ex. Local prison, high school, etc)?

(I) What would we need to do to prepare our team to support these individuals knowing they will likely be more anxious when they first join us?

24. Do we acknowledge equally the big and small gifts of time that people give us?

(I) How can we be sure to thank everyone no matter how much or how little time they give?

25. Do we have any ways that we can create margin for volunteers?

(I) Is there any way we can help interested candidates problem solve so they can join us?

26. Do we have any language in any of our documents that suggests giving money is a true sign of commitment?

    (I) What documents are given to new board members, committee members, etc that they have to read or sign?

    (II) Do any of those documents need updating to get rid of that language?

27. When we ask for specific items are we being *exact*?

(I)   Are we providing as much detail as possible?

(II) What are we asking for now?

(III) Can we be more specific in our descriptions?

28. Have we been clear about our definition of the quality of items we are asking for?

(I)   What does 'excellent condition' mean to us?

(II) What does 'good condition' mean to us?

(III) Are there any descriptions of quality associated with items we are asking for that we could benefit from clarifying?

29. Are we asking for anything that has long-term consequences associated with it?

(I)   Does it need to be moved?

(II) Will it impact our taxes or insurance rates?

(III) Are there any things we're looking at taking on that we've forgotten to consider the larger logistics around?

30. Are there any stores where we could set up a registry?

(I) Do we want to create our own registry on our website?

(II) Are there any local providers we want to consider partnering with to create a registry?

31. Do we tell people ahead of time how we will use their money or do our communications tell people what we did with it after it was spent?

(I)   What initiatives are coming up?

(II) How can we make our communications about money more future-focused rather than past tense?

32. What is our smallest need?

33. What is our biggest need?

34. What are all the other needs in between (smallest and biggest)?

35. What is the bare bones version of our organization if we hit a 10 year starvation period?

(I) How much or what do we need to keep alive in order to still exist 10 years from now if we had barely anything to work with?

(II) Do we provide products/services that earn enough to keep that bare-bones alive?

36. Can our current structure survive if the only resources we receive are from the products and services we offer?

(I) If we were never given another gift again and could only rely on fees from purchased services, could we make it?

(II) What, if anything, would have to change in order to earn our ability to exist?

37. Are we planning any expansions?

(I) Can we sustain those expansions as part of our bare bones structure or would that expansion rely on ongoing gifts from donors?

(II) Can we earn the ability to keep that expansion alive or do we need to postpone that expansion until we're in a more stable position and are not at the mercy of the market?

38. Do we have any bad choices we need to confess to our corporation or donor community?

(I) We could be exposed at any time. How do we prepare to take responsibility for our choices and actions whether we confess in time or get exposed first?

39. What do we have to offer that people can pay for (make the list as long as possible and then ask the question five more times!)

40. Are we offering products or services that are in tune with, disconnected from, or in conflict with our values and mission?

(I) Do we create an environment and an experience that help people to connect more deeply with us?

41. What makes what we have to offer of value to our donors?

(I) Do we have any crap we need to get rid of to make the bigger picture of what we have to offer higher quality?

42. Are there any campaigns on Kickstarter that seem to have similar goals or projects to ours? What kinds of rewards or gifts are they offering their donors?

43. Are we making crap?

    (I)   Do we work with any suppliers who sell crap?

    (II) How do we make sure we never buy or pass on crap ever again?

44. Do we know who the Connectors are in our donor community as opposed to the people who have volunteered their time to pass on our messages?

45. Are we specific when we tell our donor community who we are looking to connect with?

(I) Do we have any current job postings, volunteer postings, or social media shout outs that need to be updated to be specific?

46. Do we give anything back to the community that is not about us (in other words, we don't intentionally collect any resources from it)?

47. Do we ask people in our community how we can help them or offer to meet needs that we are aware of?

48. Are there any needs we know of in the community right now that could be opportunities to foster gratitude?

49. Do we give anything back to our staff/volunteers?

50. Are we giving out gifts using measurable means (*you got the best customer ratings*) or random means (*gift draw*) instead of subjective means (*you're the most positive*)?

51. Are the gifts we hand out valuable or are we giving out crap?

52. Are we using our resources to give out one or two nice things or a lot of little crappy things?

53. What systems do we have in place for confirming information such as correct spelling of names, number of volunteer hours, or relevant life details when recognizing someone?

54. Are we wasting *any of our resources* paying for crap?

   (I) Is there anything we are printing our logo on because we believed we needed to give people crap so they would remember us?

   (II) What can we actually do to *be memorable*?

(III) Can people find us easily on Google?

55. Do we give out t-shirts?

    (I)   Do they meet the four filters found in the chapter on Gratitude?

56. How can we train our current team to be in line with our resource campaigning mentality if they've previously been working with a fundraising mentality?

    (I)   How can we communicate to them how important the difference is and why we're asking them to do it this new way?

57. How can we train incoming people to be in line with our resource campaigning mentality if they are likely coming in with a fundraising background?

(I) How can we communicate to them how important the difference is and why we're asking them to do it this new way?

58. Do we have any systems of measurement we've been using to track our progress/success that are going to have to change in order to have accurate data regarding our resource campaigns (many tools that help track success for fundraisers do not carry over to resource campaigning)?

59. If I am trying to raise personal support, are there others who are trying to raise support for something similar?

(I) Would there be any benefit to banding together and trying to raise resources together rather than pursuing independent initiatives?

60. If we are an organization trying to gather resources, are there other organizations who are trying to gather resources for something similar?

(I)   Would there be any benefit to banding together and trying to gather resources together rather than pursuing independent initiatives?

61. Are there any other organizations that we have been viewing as competition for resources?

(I)   Is there value to us exploring a partnership with those organizations?

(II) What would happen if we combined our resources?

(III) What would happen if we simply stopped seeing them as competition?

62. Do we have any events we've been offering that are only geared towards specific age groups (ex. Seniors or children)?

    (I)   Would there be any benefit to opening up the age range or even including more generations?

63. Are there any places in my personal life where I can start to apply a resource campaign mentality?

(I) Would practicing the principles for myself have any impact on how I try to apply the principles for the organization I'm a part of?

64. Are there any new initiatives/events/etc we could pursue that would help to increase the number of people we connect with?

(I) How could we build connections with new people?

(II) How could we deepen our relationship with people who we are already connected to?

65. Do we know which of our donors have given to us in the form of multiple resource categories?

66. Do we know which of our donors has a tendency to give more strongly from one specific resource category?

67. Do I have a primary way of giving when asked for help, or do I tend to give in the form of multiple resource categories?

68. Are there any donors we've had a strong relationship with in the past that we haven't heard from recently?

(I) Is there a way we can check in with them, not to ask for anything, but to just reconnect and find out how they are doing?

(II) Is there anything that happened to cause a break in our relationship that would benefit from being addressed?

If you want to go all out with a major effort within a larger organization, bringing together a number of people to enact bigger change, then I can suggest taking the following steps.

STEP 1: GATHERING YOUR TEAM

In order to create a comprehensive resource campaign, you need to gather the right people at the same table. If you are spread out geographically, this conversation is going to be worth trying to meet in person for!

Who do you need to gather together? Who is in charge of:

- Finances
- Fundraising
- Human Resources
- Volunteer Recruitment
- Property Management
- Inventory Management
- Product Delivery or Program Services
- Communications
- Events Planning

I'm going to refer to this group of people as your resource campaign's Core Team. *Before* your Core Team meets I highly recommend establishing communication channels within your organization that let every other member of the team contribute to a Master List of needs and wants in order to have an accurate picture of what you're trying to achieve with your resource campaign. Trust me, there are some insightful surprises waiting for you if this Master List is created before your Core Team meets!

Try sending out a message to everyone within your organization, or the key players who manage the internal teams, with the following:

We are exploring trying a new initiative and need your insight. Could you tell us what needs you see within our organization, gaps that need to be filled or things that need to be replaced/repaired in the next 10 years? We'd also love to know if you could have anything to help you better accomplish our organization's mission or help us to reach further, what would you need or want? Thank you for your input!

See what you get back and have the Master List, the compilation of all the responses, available to your Core Team when they meet to discuss entering this new campaigning era.

STEP 2: SORT THE WANTS AND NEEDS

Have the Core Team break down the list of wants and needs they personally are aware of into The 6 Key Resource Categories. Next break down the wants and needs from the Master List into The 6 Key Resource Categories adding them to the items your Core Team already wrote down. Ask for each item *could this need be met with money, volunteered time/skills, specific items, purchased services, connections, or gratitude* and note where needed if the item in question could be fulfilled in multiple ways.

With this 'wants and needs' map laid out in front of you, there might be some much-needed insight into the bigger picture of your organization's current resources and where people are seeing gaps or opportunity for growth. This will be excellent food for thought for the Core Team members as they see what items more specifically fall under their umbrella. They may even discover needs they weren't aware of because there had previously been no reason or means before to communicate with the person who needed it. Organizations have to get past the outdated idea of the 'if you need it you tell *me*' mentality that often means there are levels of management in between the person who needs a resource and the person who can actually get it for them. If this communication structure is interfering with your organization's ability to get the right things to the right people then this exercise can also help with making policy changes or structural changes to make things flow more freely and in a more timely manner.

STEP 3: IDENTIFY YOUR BARE BONES STRUCTURE AND NEEDS TO KEEP IT ALIVE

Mentally place your organization in a ten-year starvation scenario. Resources are going to dry up. There will only be scraps to work with. If you want to still exist ten years from now when a time of feasting returns then where do you need to channel your limited resources during the famine?

Look back at the list of wants and needs that have been placed on your radar. Look for items that are bare bones items. You may not have realized that a building needs to be re-shingled two years from now, that a specific license has to be renewed every five years, or that an expensive dishwasher in the cafeteria is going to bite the dust any day now and needs to be replaced to continue operations.

With your Core Team at the table, there may be some eye-opening moments as to what your organization actually requires at the bare minimum to sustain itself now and in that ten year period coming up. We have what under our building? We pay that much to the city? That's how much we're paying for hydro? The insurance for that program is what? The interest payments are what? We have to renew that every three years?

Don't assume your financial expert can answer this question on their own. Any number of times the spreadsheet they look at is broken down into budget lines. They may see the receipts, invoices, and totals, but that doesn't mean that they know what all the priority must-have items are that comprise the bare bones structure. It's in partnership, as a larger team, that the bare bones picture and the answer to how much it costs to keep it alive will more accurately be answered.

STEP 4: CAN YOU SUSTAIN YOUR BARE BONES?

Look at what products and services your organization offers and what kind of revenue they bring in. Does the revenue cover the costs of keeping the bare bones alive? If the answer is yes, great, move on to Step 5. If the answer is no, you need to fix that problem now.

If there is an obvious answer that you can see to fix the problem, run with that. If there are no obvious answers for how to increase income to cover bare-bones expenses then have everyone on the Core Team grab a piece of paper and a pen. Everyone has 10 minutes to brainstorm individually and write down what products or services your organization could offer that would bring in the resources needed to sustain the bare bones.

When the 10 minutes is up, have people gather together into groups of 3-5 (this might be your whole Core Team) and share what they came up with. Then as a group ask the question 'what else could we do' five times and add the five answers that team comes up with to the list in hand. If you had multiple small groups bring everyone together for a final comparison of notes. If creative juices still seem to be flowing you can keep asking 'what else can we do', and then take stock of the final amalgamated list. How do you want to move forward and what do you need to do to make that happen?

Sometimes a fix requires relatively little time or effort. It just took intentional time spent focused on the issue to identify a course of action for change. Other times a yawning gap has presented itself and the solution is going to take time. Instead of minor course correction, you are having to chart a new course entirely and do a lot of planning to prepare for the voyage. That's okay. Don't be intimidated or discouraged by that revelation or the process ahead. What would have been worse is if you'd kept going down the path you were on. It's much better to put muscle into steering the ship towards a sunny horizon, then to keep your boat sailing smoothly towards the rocks.

STEP 5: EXPLORE HOW ROLES AND COMMUNICATION STRUCTURES MIGHT CHANGE

When the request for resources, rather than funds, goes public and the resources start pouring in, how are they going to be managed? If someone wants to donate something big, who needs to know about it and coordinate its arrival? Who needs to communicate when a need has been met in one way or another and who do they tell (this is especially important for items that could be fulfilled in multiple ways)? What partnerships outside of the organization need to be developed? What documents need to be reviewed to weed out old fundraising language and who is going to review them? This is a big shift! Fundraising for years carves a sort of groove for an organization to follow and it can be hard work climbing out of the groove in order to do something new, but the effort is so absolutely worth it!

STEP 6: GO!

Start releasing your initial communications using your new resource campaign language that reflects The 6 Key Resource Categories. If you're sending out e-newsletters consider using a template that looks something like this:

- Current events (include both triumphs and challenges!)
- Here's what we have to offer that you can pay for…
- We need the following specific items…
- We're looking for people to…
- We're looking for financial support to reach further…
- We're looking to connect with these people…
- Here's how we're giving back (community events, scholarships, draws for prizes, etc)

- Spread the word!

If you're using social media then try rotating through these categories. Tweet about a triumph today and a challenge tomorrow. Ask for volunteers on Monday, funds on Wednesday, and celebrate Scavenger Hunt Fridays with a request for help finding a specific item your team needs each week. You get the idea. When you have a limited number of characters to work with it can be a good idea to focus on a single thing per post and keep changing up your focus with each post to equally cover all your bases.

If you have canvassers going door-to-door or volunteers who make phone calls then prepare them with conversation starters and the goal to Connect! Connect! Connect! Have written lists of your organization's various needs so that as their conversations go in various directions they can always refer back to the sheet or document to see if there is a need that might resonate with this particular donor.

Update your website! Update your app! If you have partners who try to communicate your needs and do campaigning on your behalf be sure to tell them the news about your new initiatives and language and help them to get on board.

STEP 7: SHARE YOUR SUCCESS STORIES!

Could you do me a favour? When you see the amazing things that resource campaigning is doing for your organization, would you please share your story with me and the broader resource campaign community? It makes me stupidly happy to hear when someone is celebrating a breakthrough and I'd love to cheer you on and be celebrating on your behalf too. And it would be amazing for people to be able to hear what's working for you or lessons you've learned along the way. Old fundraising mentality would have taught you that other organizations were the competition also trying to get people's money, but now we know we're a complex community with room for everyone and plenty of resources to go around. You can share by hopping on Facebook and finding the group Resource Campaign Community.

16

CONCLUSION

You may have noticed that the math in this book doesn't quite add up…

CONCLUSION

You may have noticed that the math in this book doesn't quite add up. We now know that any given person you connect with wants to give to you from one of The 6 Key Resource Categories and that communities are made up of balanced numbers of people who want to give from each category based on who you are and what you are asking for. This means if you connect with a community and ask for something from only one category you will get a response from 1/6. 1/6 is 1 divided by 6 which equals 0.1666666666 or 17%. Reverse engineer that equation and multiply 17% by 6 and you get 102%.

That is actually my wish for you and your organization. That, while it looks a little off at first, if you put resource campaigning into motion for your organization that the end result will be receiving 102% of everything you wanted and needed to make the world a better place.

If you're interested in continuing the conversation about resource campaigning please join the Facebook group Resource Campaign Community and share your thoughts or learn from other people's successes.

And if you want to get in touch with me about team building programs, speaking engagements, or training to support what your organization is doing I'd love to hear from you. Hop on over to www.opendoordevelopment.ca and you can get in touch with me through the email and phone number posted there.

Wishing you all the best,

Lindsay Walton

APPENDIX A:
A NOTE FOR CHURCHES

APPENDIX A: A NOTE FOR CHURCHES

There is something I want to clarify for anyone who grabbed this book for a church. This book will be very beneficial to anyone who is interested in seeing resources distributed as needed throughout the Body of Christ, the global Church, similar to what is seen in the book of Acts in the bible. Less so if the principles are applied to meet the needs of a single church gathering registered under the banner of a unique non-profit entity.

The Church (big C) is not a non-profit. Individual gatherings of people may choose to register with the government to obtain non-profit status as a church (small c), but doing so has farther reaching outcomes than many realize. There are many ways that non-profit regulations make their way into everyday church structure and operations, creating intense confusion about what God is asking people to do and what the government is asking people to do. These include, but are not limited to:

- Membership (you are now part of the non-profit's Corporation)

- Annual general meetings (a requirement for communicating with the Corporation)

- Voting (a requirement for the Corporation to submit input)

- The term "Board" of Elders/Deacons (the Board is the group legally and financially on the hook if the non-profit ship goes down...)

- Forcing identification with a denomination (a required identifier to complete a non-profit application) instead of simply identifying as a member of the Church

- Having to affiliate with an overseeing body for that denomination (a requirement of being able to identify with it on a non-profit application) which often requires a financial commitment to that overseeing body

- Meeting under multitudes of names (you can not name your non-profit the same thing as another registered non-profit)

- Meeting under multitudes of symbols (you can not use the same logo as another registered non-profit)

You'll also want to watch out because your contact information will be made publicly available. The government list of registered non-profits is harvested by organizations wanting to sell them products. Many products are rebranded for churches by organizations who think churches are humanitarian groups or community halls. For example, resources to help churches encourage higher levels of 'giving'. The tools, designed to increase donations, don't distinguish between a gift to a non-profit and a gift to God so they just use the word 'giving' or substitute the word 'tithing' for 'donation' while missing the heart behind the idea. They're focused on selling you a product. It may not be a bad thing, the tool could be very useful, but it can also have unintended side effects.

I'm sharing all this here because I have seen the long-term outcomes of communities divided and people pulling away from God when they can't see the difference between being in a relationship with God and belonging to a world-wide Body, and going through the motions of building individual, thriving non-profits that are based on Jesus. Those things can blur more easily than you would think.

For anyone who is thinking about 'planting a church', I will provide the following thought for consideration. Jesus started the Church. If you would like to establish a smaller gathering of people who belong to that global Body you would be wise to explore what other alternatives you have to registering that group for non-profit status. If your gathering is already registered as a non-profit, it could be worth asking what would need to be done to change your status and asking how things might change if the government no longer had a say in how things must be structured or function.

[For anyone who believes a gathering of people benefit from registering as a non-profit because it provides financial accountability and reduces the chances of someone using tithing fraudulently, I asked a friend of mine who investigates these kinds of cases, and he laughed. His stance is that people are still people. Registering for non-profit status will not stop someone in a church from choosing to commit fraud.]

> *Now the full number of those who believed were of one heart and soul, and no one said that any of the things that belonged to him was his own, but they had everything in common. And with great power the apostles were giving their testimony to the resurrection of the Lord Jesus, and great grace was upon them all. There was not a needy person among them, for as many as were owners of lands or houses sold them and brought the proceeds of what was sold and laid it at the apostles' feet, and it was distributed to each as any had need.*
>
> ~ Acts 4:32-35

APPENDIX B:

Does Your Non-Profit Need To Be A Non-Profit?

Groups of people gathered to take on a challenge of some kind in our
world often register for non-profit status simply because they believe it's
what they need to do. But that's not always the case.

It is worth the time to consider whether or not your particular gathering of
people can change the world in the way you hope to change it through a
for-profit model or through just *being*.

In a for-profit model your group would need to have a valuable product or
service that you offer which people would be willing to pay for and a
sustainable business model that would provide for your needs to exist (this
may or may not include salaries depending on whether your group wants to
volunteer or be paid to dedicate their time). No matter what your cause
there will always be something of value you can offer that is in line with
your values and purpose that people are willing to pay for. You don't have
to earn money so that you can go make the world a better place. You can
earn money in such a way that the world is made a better place while you
earn.

Groups interested in supporting the homeless can create homeless survival
packs that are backpacks filled with basic necessities for survival and feeling
like a human being. They can sell these kits to people who either want to
hand deliver the pack to a homeless person they are aware of in their
community, or to people who would prefer your group deliver it to
someone in need. It's okay to say that people will not receive a charitable
receipt for their purchase!

Groups interested in supporting environmental health can hire themselves
out for local clean-up projects. Groups wanting to support homeless
animals can provide paid animal grooming services and use the profits to
pay for veterinary services and foster care for homeless animals.

My company, Open Door Development, provides team building programs
and training in specific team skills including conflict resolution, stress
reduction, and first aid training. Organizations pay to have us come to their
site to provide programs and training that radically impacts the participants'
ability to work together and increases both their length of life and quality
of life. We get regular feedback from participants that what they learned
during their time with us made a big difference which they are incredibly
grateful for. That makes my heart want to burst on a regular basis because I
started the company in the first place with the goal of ensuring no human

being ever feels alone while navigating life's challenges. That is a horrible feeling and no one should ever have to feel that way *ever*. I could fill out grant applications and do fundraisers and collect donations to try and get the money needed to go and train as many people as possible in the team skills that will make their lives better and our teams and communities stronger, or I could ask people to pay. And people do. I and my team are out in the world making it a better place, pursuing changing the world in the ways that we are most passionate about, and being paid to do so.

In a just-being model a group of people can treat pursuing their goal or mission as just being part of Life. It's not something they take time out of their schedules to do. It's just a part of living and for that reason they go with the flow and make use of or find resources as needed without needing to create some kind of formal structure. A group of people wanting to run safe after-school programs for youth in dangerous neighbourhoods can go and do exactly that. A group of people wanting to use their expertise to dig wells in communities without safe and reliable access to water can go and do exactly that.

If you are already a registered non-profit it is worth the time to stop and think about whether or not that is the best model for you to be operating in. Think through the scenarios. The thing you are trying to do, the change you want to achieve, the principles you want to embody and live, and what would it look like if you were trying to achieve those things through a for-profit model? Or what would it look like if you were trying to achieve those things by just living your life?

If your brain gets stuck, or a little leprechaun pops up on your shoulder and says, "You can't do that", tell him to take a hike and go find a trusted sounding board to bounce your thoughts off of or a trusted expert to find out their perspective. Something that is a better fit might be waiting for you.

APPENDIX C:
Resource Campaign Conversation Starters

APPENDIX C: RESOURCE CAMPAIGN CONVERSATION STARTERS

Hello!

My name is [insert name] and I'm with [insert name of organization]. We [insert purpose or mission] and are looking for help gathering the resources we need to achieve our mission!

We offer [insert Purchased Service/Product you offer and how to pay]. We are looking for several items including [insert 1-3 Specific Items you are looking for] and are also looking for volunteers to [insert Volunteering positions you are trying to fill]. We collect financial donations as [insert methods you use for collecting Money] and are looking to connect with [insert any Connections you are trying to find]. Is there anything I've shared that is of interest to you, or that might be of interest to someone else you know?

Thank you so much for your time and help! Before I go I'll just let you know that we [insert what you are doing to foster Gratitude in your community or say you would love to help them and ask if there is anything you can give them a hand with.]

Hello!

My name is [insert name] and I'm with [insert name of organization]. We [insert purpose or mission] and are looking for help gathering the six categories of resources we need to achieve our mission!

We are looking for people who would be interested in purchasing our services/products, helping us find specific items we need, volunteering, giving money, helping us connect with specific people, and for people in our community that we can help. If you tell me which of those categories sounds of most interest to you I would be happy to tell you more!

APPENDIX D:
Resource Campaign Scavenger Hunt Template

A fun way to gather resources is to have a Scavenger Hunt event where people are sent out into the community as individuals, in pairs, or small groups to try and gather all the items from their list. For example, a group of 50 people, broken down into 25 pairs, are each given a scavenger hunt form (see next page) and 3 hours to try and find everything on their list. At the end of the three hours they must return to a designated location where the final tally will be completed and the group with the most items awarded a prize!

There are any number of ways to go about organizing an event like this so this is simply a jumping off point, but check out the sample scavenger hunt sheet on the next page and let your imagination play with the possibilities for your organization!

Note: If you have tickets to an upcoming event, send the group out with the tickets and make it a scavenger hunt item to find people who will purchase them!

Because this book has been about respecting resources, gathering and using them wisely, nothing on the list is random and will therefore turn into waste. For the purpose of this exercise we will assume that the scavenger hunt is collecting resources for a summer camp serving at-risk youth and that every item on the list has an intended purpose. Even if an item doesn't make sense at first glance, we'll assume the organization knows exactly what it needs that resource for.

[Note: The following scavenger hunt list is being handed out to 25 groups of 2. That means that it would be possible to end up with each of those items x25. It's a good idea to do scavenger hunts for things you need a lot of!]

SCAVENGER HUNT!

❑❑❑❑❑5 pens	❑ pack of cue cards
❑1 kiddie pool	❑ pack of playing cards
❑ 1 ball of yarn	❑❑ 2 cans crushed tomatoes
❑ 1 set of knitting needles	❑❑ 2 cans of soup
❑ 1 set of crochet hooks	❑ 1 towel
❑ 1 multipurpose screwdriver	❑ 1 roll duct tape
❑❑❑❑❑❑❑❑❑❑ 10 people to attend our guest speaker event (tickets $25 each)	❑ 1 volunteer to help serve food at our BBQ fundraiser on July 27 from 10am–2pm at Eden Park.
❑❑❑❑❑ 5 tennis balls	❑ 1 block of sticky notes
❑ 1 pack of printer paper (8.5x11)	❑❑ 2 neck ties
❑❑ 2 children's books	❑ 1 ugly sweater
❑ 1 bucket	❑ 1 umbrella
❑ 1 pair rubber boots (any size)	❑❑ 2 packs of garden seeds (for any plant)
❑ 1 rain jacket/poncho (any size)	❑❑ 2 plant pots (any size)
❑ 1 compass	❑ 1 garden tool (any kind)
❑❑❑❑❑ 5 Loonies	❑ 1 hand mirror
❑❑❑❑❑ 5 Toonies	❑ 1 musical instrument (any kind)
❑❑❑❑ 4 $5 dollar bills	❑ 1 keychain
❑❑❑❑ 4 $10 dollar bills	❑ 1 $25 gas gift certificate (any gas station)
❑❑❑❑ 4 $20 dollar bills	❑ 1 new pair shoelaces
❑❑ 2 $50 dollar bills	❑❑❑❑❑ 5 plain envelopes
❑ $100 dollar bill	❑❑❑❑❑❑❑❑❑❑ 10 high fives

Share your feedback and requests!

If you have ideas for tools that should be created or feedback regarding how the value of this book could be increased to organizations, communities, and individuals who want to know more about resource campaigning, please send your suggestions to:

myideas@opendoordevelopment.ca

Thank you for your contribution!!!

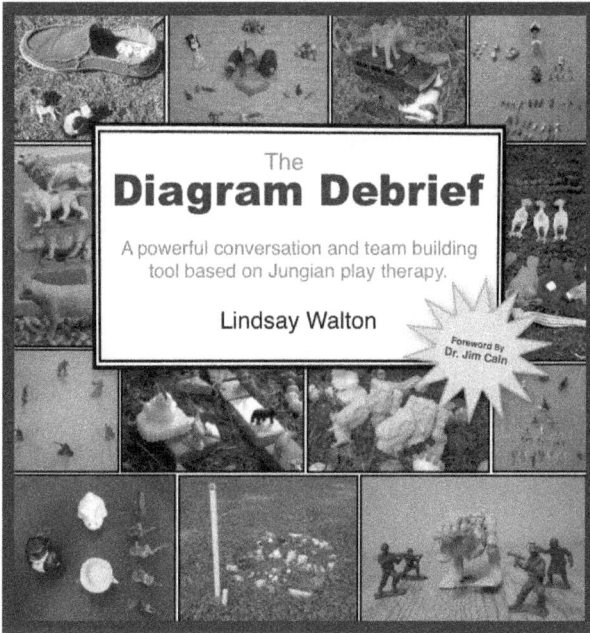

The
Diagram Debrief

A powerful conversation and team building
tool based on Jungian play therapy.

Lindsay Walton

Foreword By
Dr. Jim Cain

Fun and incredibly insightful, the Diagram Debrief is a tool that helps people to start a conversation with their teammates and with themselves! You can gain insight into who has influence, where connection and disconnection exist, characteristics of individual team members, the nature of relationships between teammates, as well as challenges to navigate or things to celebrate!

Intended for use with teams in all of their glorious variety you can do everything from asking your staff to make a picture of their work team, to asking your children to make a picture of your family or your students to make a picture of their school.

In this book you will find step by step directions for facilitating the Diagram Debrief, suggested questions for exploring completed diagrams, recommendations on how to build your own Diagram Debrief kit and more!

Available for purchase at Amazon and
www.opendoordevelopment.ca/shop.

ISBN: 978-1-7753276-2-2

www.ingramcontent.com/pod-product-compliance
Lightning Source LLC
Chambersburg PA
CBHW031404180326
41458CB00043B/6611/J